# Approaches to learning and teaching

# Science

## a toolkit for international teachers

**Mark Winterbottom and
James de Winter**

Series Editors: Paul Ellis and Lauren Harris

# CAMBRIDGE
## UNIVERSITY PRESS

University Printing House, Cambridge CB2 8BS, United Kingdom

One Liberty Plaza, 20th Floor, New York, NY 10006, USA

477 Williamstown Road, Port Melbourne, VIC 3207, Australia

314–321, 3rd Floor, Plot 3, Splendor Forum, Jasola District Centre, New Delhi – 110025, India

79 Anson Road, #06–04/06, Singapore 079906

Cambridge University Press is part of the University of Cambridge.

It furthers the University's mission by disseminating knowledge in the pursuit of education, learning and research at the highest international levels of excellence.

www.cambridge.org
Information on this title: www.cambridge.org/9781316645857 (Paperback)

© Cambridge International Examinations 2017

First published 2017

20  19  18  17  16  15  14  13  12  11  10  9  8  7  6  5  4  3  2  1

Printed in Great Britain by CPI Group (UK) Ltd, Croydon CR0 4YY

*A catalogue record for this publication is available from the British Library*

ISBN  978-1-316-64585-7  Paperback

# Contents

| | | |
|---|---|---|
| Acknowledgements | | iv |
| 1 | Introduction to the series by the editors | 1 |
| 2 | Purpose and context | 4 |
| 3 | The nature of the subject | 8 |
| 4 | Key considerations | 16 |
| 5 | Interpreting a syllabus | 24 |
| 6 | Active learning | 30 |
| 7 | Assessment for Learning | 43 |
| 8 | Metacognition | 55 |
| 9 | Language awareness | 69 |
| 10 | Inclusive education | 85 |
| 11 | Teaching with digital technologies | 101 |
| 12 | Global thinking | 116 |
| 13 | Reflective practice | 131 |
| 14 | Understanding the impact of classroom practice on student progress | 139 |
| Recommended reading | | 149 |
| Index | | 153 |

Online lesson ideas for this book can be found at
cambridge.org/9781316645857

# Acknowledgements

*The authors and publishers acknowledge the following sources of copyright material and are grateful for the permissions granted. While every effort has been made, it has not always been possible to identify the sources of all the material used, or to trace all copyright holders. If any omissions are brought to our notice, we will be happy to include the appropriate acknowledgements on reprinting.*

Cover image: bgblue/Getty Images; Inside: Fig. 10.1 Jack Hollingsworth/Getty Images; Fig. 11.1 Gail Webdell; Fig. 11.2, 11.3 and 11.4 James de Winter; Fig. 12.1 Thomas Barwick/Getty Images; Online Lesson idea 11.4 James de Winter

# Introduction to the series by the editors

1

# 1 Approaches to learning and teaching Science

This series of books is the result of close collaboration between Cambridge University Press and Cambridge International Examinations, both departments of the University of Cambridge. The books are intended as a companion guide for teachers, to supplement your learning and provide you with extra resources for the lessons you are planning. Their focus is deliberately not syllabus-specific, although occasional reference has been made to programmes and qualifications. We want to invite you to set aside for a while assessment objectives and grading, and take the opportunity instead to look in more depth at how you teach your subject and how you motivate and engage with your students.

The themes presented in these books are informed by evidence-based research into what works to improve students' learning and pedagogical best practices. To ensure that these books are first and foremost practical resources, we have chosen not to include too many academic references, but we have provided some suggestions for further reading.

We have further enhanced the books by asking the authors to create accompanying lesson ideas. These are described in the text and can be found in a dedicated space online. We hope the books will become a dynamic and valid representation of what is happening now in learning and teaching in the context in which you work.

Our organisations also offer a wide range of professional development opportunities for teachers. These range from syllabus- and topic-specific workshops and large-scale conferences to suites of accredited qualifications for teachers and school leaders. Our aim is to provide you with valuable support, to build communities and networks, and to help you both enrich your own teaching methodology and evaluate its impact on your students.

Each of the books in this series follows a similar structure. In the first chapter, we have asked our authors to consider the essential elements of their subject, the main concepts that might be covered in a school curriculum, and why these are important. The next chapter gives you a brief guide on how to interpret a syllabus or subject guide, and how to plan a programme of study. The authors will encourage you to think too about what is not contained in a syllabus and how you can pass on your own passion for the subject you teach.

The main body of the text takes you through those aspects of learning and teaching which are widely recognised as important. We would like to stress that there is no single recipe for excellent teaching, and that different schools, operating in different countries and cultures, will have strong traditions that should be respected. There is a growing consensus, however, about some important practices and approaches that need to be adopted if students are going to fulfil their potential and be prepared for modern life.

In the common introduction to each of these chapters we look at what the research says and the benefits and challenges of particular approaches. Each author then focuses on how to translate theory into practice in the context of their subject, offering practical lesson ideas and teacher tips. These chapters are not mutually exclusive but can be read independently of each other and in whichever order suits you best. They form a coherent whole but are presented in such a way that you can dip into the book when and where it is most convenient for you to do so.

The final two chapters are common to all the books in this series and are not written by the subject authors. Schools and educational organisations are increasingly interested in the impact that classroom practice has on student outcomes. We have therefore included an exploration of this topic and some practical advice on how to evaluate the success of the learning opportunities you are providing for your students. The book then closes with some guidance on how to reflect on your teaching and some avenues you might explore to develop your own professional learning.

We hope you find these books accessible and useful. We have tried to make them conversational in tone so you feel we are sharing good practice rather than directing it. Above all, we hope that the books will inspire you and enable you to think in more depth about how you teach and how your students learn.

Paul Ellis and Lauren Harris

Series Editors

# 2 | Purpose and context

International research into educational effectiveness tells us that student achievement is influenced most by what teachers do in classrooms. In a world of rankings and league tables we tend to notice performance, not preparation, yet the product of education is more than just examinations and certification. Education is also about the formation of effective learning habits that are crucial for success within and beyond the taught curriculum.

The purpose of this series of books is to inspire you as a teacher to reflect on your practice, try new approaches and better understand how to help your students learn. We aim to help you develop your teaching so that your students are prepared for the next level of their education as well as life in the modern world.

This book will encourage you to examine the processes of learning and teaching, not just the outcomes. We will explore a variety of teaching strategies to enable you to select which is most appropriate for your students and the context in which you teach. When you are making your choice, involve your students: all the ideas presented in this book will work best if you engage your students, listen to what they have to say, and consistently evaluate their needs.

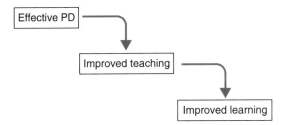

Cognitive psychologists, coaches and sports writers have noted how the aggregation of small changes can lead to success at the highest level. As teachers, we can help our students make marginal gains by guiding them in their learning, encouraging them to think and talk about how they are learning, and giving them the tools to monitor their success. If you take care of the learning, the performance will take care of itself.

When approaching an activity for the first time, or revisiting an area of learning, ask yourself if your students know how to:

- Approach a new task and plan which strategies they will use
- Monitor their progress and adapt their approach if necessary
- Look back and reflect on how well they did and what they might do differently next time.

# 2 Approaches to learning and teaching Science

Effective learners understand that learning is an active process. We need to challenge and stretch our students and enable them to interrogate, analyse and evaluate what they see and hear. Consider whether your students:

- Challenge assumptions and ask questions
- Try new ideas and take intellectual risks
- Devise strategies to overcome any barriers to their learning that they encounter.

As we discuss in the chapters on **Active learning** and **Metacognition**, it is our role as teachers to encourage these practices with our students so that they become established routines. We can help students review their own progress as well as getting a snapshot ourselves of how far they are progressing by using some of the methods we explore in the chapter on **Assessment for Learning**.

Students often view the subject lessons they are attending as separate from each other, but they can gain a great deal if we encourage them to take a more holistic appreciation of what they are learning. This requires not only understanding how various concepts in a subject fit together, but also how to make connections between different areas of knowledge and how to transfer skills from one discipline to another. As our students successfully integrate disciplinary knowledge, they are better able to solve complex problems, generate new ideas and interpret the world around them.

In order for students to construct an understanding of the world and their significance in it, we need to lead students into thinking habitually about why a topic is important on a personal, local and global scale. Do they realise the implications of what they are learning and what they do with their knowledge and skills, not only for themselves but also for their neighbours and the wider world? To what extent can they recognise and express their own perspective as well as the perspectives of others? We will consider how to foster local and global awareness, as well as personal and social responsibility, in the chapter on **Global thinking**.

As part of the learning process, some students will discover barriers to their learning: we need to recognise these and help students to overcome them. Even students who regularly meet success face their own challenges. We have all experienced barriers to our own learning at some point in our lives and should be able as teachers to empathise and share our own methods for dealing with these. In the chapter on **Inclusive education** we discuss how to make learning accessible for everyone and how to ensure that all students receive the instruction and support they need to succeed as learners.

Some students are learning through the medium of English when it is not their first language, while others may struggle to understand subject jargon even if they might otherwise appear fluent. For all students, whether they are learning through their first language or an additional language, language is a vehicle for learning. It is through language that students access the content of the lesson and communicate their ideas. So, as teachers, it is our responsibility to make sure that language isn't a barrier to learning. In the chapter on **Language awareness** we look at how teachers can pay closer attention to language to ensure that all students can access the content of a lesson.

Alongside a greater understanding of what works in education and why, we as teachers can also seek to improve how we teach and expand the tools we have at our disposal. For this reason, we have included a chapter in this book on **Teaching with digital technologies**, discussing what this means for our classrooms and for us as teachers. Institutes of higher education and employers want to work with students who are effective communicators and who are information literate. Technology brings both advantages and challenges and we invite you to reflect on how to use it appropriately.

This book has been written to help you think harder about the impact of your teaching on your students' learning. It is up to you to set an example for your students and to provide them with opportunities to celebrate success, learn from failure and, ultimately, to succeed.

We hope you will share what you gain from this book with other teachers and that you will be inspired by the ideas that are presented here. We hope that you will encourage your school leaders to foster a positive environment that allows both you and your students to meet with success and to learn from mistakes when success is not immediate. We hope too that this book can help in the creation and continuation of a culture where learning and teaching are valued and through which we can discover together what works best for each and every one of our students.

# 3 | The nature of the subject

# What is the place of Science in the curriculum?

It is easy to think of Science as a pre-formed collection of facts to be delivered to our students. However, even though there are curricular demands (they need to know stuff!), our students also need to know what Science is, and why we study it.

Learning Science should ensure that students realise the importance of evidence in making decisions and coming to conclusions, not just about scientific issues, but about social and ethical issues too.

---

**Teacher Tip**

Including ethical decision-making into learning activities in Science lessons can be very engaging for students. Try to frame a lesson around an ethical dilemma which students can only resolve after having learnt the relevant Science. For example, understanding pre-implantation genetic diagnosis can provide a framework for understanding inheritance.

---

Unless students understand how scientific knowledge is generated, through critical evaluation of evidence, they really will be simply learning a set of pre-formed facts. Most Science teachers would uphold the principle of experimental and inquiry-based learning in Science, which provides that focus on evidence. It also cultivates skills such as observation, comparison, classification and prediction. It helps students to understand how to test ideas systematically, and how to seek and interpret evidence for scientific claims.

Are these skills necessarily superior to those taught by other subjects? Not really. But are they important in a world focused on scientific development, where science and technology are fundamental components of many economies? Yes, of course!

---

Teacher Tip

Discuss with teachers of History how they introduce inquiry and evidence in their lessons. Gaining perspectives from a different subject which also focuses on evidence can help you to think about your own practice in developing students' inquiry skills.

---

However, Science has something more natural underpinning it. You can think of every child as a mini-scientist. They have spent their childhood trying to make sense of the world, drawing upon observations of natural phenomena. But that process isn't perfect, and may leave the children with misconceptions (sometimes known as alternative conceptions), even if such misconceptions may have a small amount of 'truth' within them!

For example, children may suggest that wrapping a blanket around a block of ice would make it melt quicker, because when the blanket is wrapped around their body, it feels warm. Likewise, when they are asked to draw arrows between an object and an eye, to help describe how sight happens, children will often draw arrows pointing towards the object. This idea of 'active eyes' makes sense to children, but having understood the Science, they would direct the arrows correctly, showing the passage of light from the object to the eye.

Replacing intuitive 'sense-making' with systematic 'sense-making' is one of the primary purposes of Science education, promoting systematic and critical thinking in your students.

---

# What are some of the fundamental areas of knowledge in Science?

In many schools, and by many teachers, school Science tends to be thought of simply as a body of knowledge. If this is you, don't worry; you're not alone. You probably found Science fascinating as a child, and you simply want to pass on these fascinating ideas to your students.

That body of knowledge is usually split into Physics, Chemistry and Biology, and can also include social sciences such as Psychology. It contains facts, definitions, laws and other ideas which have been tested and accepted by the scientific community. Once they have been accepted, they become part of a school Science syllabus and textbook. Physics includes ideas about waves, energy, electricity and forces. Chemistry includes ideas about reactions, particles, acids and bases. Biology includes ideas about cell biology, human biology, plant biology, evolution, genetics, ecology and conservation.

However, Science also includes knowledge about the methods and processes of Science touched on earlier, such as observing, measuring, predicting, hypothesising, experimenting and so on. It is these skills that we frequently overlook as teachers, choosing to focus on knowledge, even when they are in fact given importance by examination specifications, and teaching them can contribute directly to our education of a new generation of scientists. Designing data collection, analysing data, controlling variables and ensuring repeatability are common skills across the scientific disciplines, and it is these common themes that draw the sciences together.

Hence, this body of knowledge and these skills contribute to students' understanding of Science as a way of knowing. Here there are key ideas such as scientific knowledge being based on evidence, scientific knowledge changing over time in response to new evidence, and the role creativity, cooperation and collaboration play in the development of new scientific ideas. Students should also encounter the diversity of scientific thinking, the way in which scientific knowledge has been developed historically and the importance of asking questions.

---

**Teacher Tip**

Audit your teaching to see if it really contributes to students' understanding of Science as a way of knowing. Identify two things you could change in your most recent lesson to reduce students' impression that Science is just a body of facts.

---

It is our mission as teachers to help students understand and remember a body of knowledge, but it's equally important to develop our students' skills as scientists, and students' understanding of how Science works as its own way of knowing and thinking.

# What makes a good scientist?

Isaac Asimov said that the most exciting phrase to hear in science was not 'Eureka', heralding a new discovery, but 'Hmm ... that's funny'. Buckminster Fuller said that he would give only average grades to all the 'parrots' who told him the right answer, but he would give the top grades to the students who made lots of mistakes and told him what they'd learnt from the mistakes.

Both give a sense that scientists should always be learning, that scientists never stop seeking new knowledge and that scientists are addicted to questions. Indeed, Edward Wilson, in his *Letters to a Young Scientist*, went further. He advised his students to daydream but work hard. He stressed the creativity and entrepreneurship required to be a good scientist. He pointed out that good scientists are people who enjoy messing around with things, doing quick uncontrolled experiments, until they notice something nobody else has seen. When they notice it, they ask 'why' and 'how'.

---

### Teacher Tip

Begin a lesson with a demonstration, and ask students to think of a question to follow each of the following 'question words': *what?, when?, why?, how?*

---

Science makes progress when we find data that contradicts our current scientific ideas. Good scientists are always asking why things happen or how things happen. By asking questions like this, they are able to come up with new theories to explain new findings, and then test those theories. Scientific ideas can never be said to be proven: every idea is potentially falsifiable if the data eventually contradicts it. But learning how to ask 'how' and 'why' seems fundamental to educating our students.

So how do we give our students the sense that they are doing Science, and the opportunity to experience Science and become better scientists? Underpinning students' learning with practical and experimental inquiries can be a good approach. Encouraging students to ask questions, formulate hypotheses, decide what evidence to collect, analyse it and make conclusions are fundamental to what scientists do; not in a formulaic way to satisfy an examination board, but in a natural and authentic way in a real inquiry. Of course, students cannot always choose the focus for their own inquiries – you've got a syllabus to teach! But the more we encourage student autonomy, the better scientists they will become.

This gives a rather ideal picture of a good scientist. Most scientists would tell you that scientific research can be a little boring when collecting research data. They can tell you about tens and hundreds of experiments that went wrong, and data that was impossible to collect. So you need resilience as a scientist to handle the obstacles; you need to develop strategies to think your way around the obstacles; and while aiming for perfection, you must be able to settle for excellence.

# Why is Science important to me?

My own journey as a scientist began at Oxford University, where I studied Zoology. As part of my degree, I undertook an honours project on why pheasants crow. In those days, although I had done a lot of practical work, I hadn't really been taught how to plan a research project. The question had been given to me by my supervisor, and I arrived at the Game Conservancy in Hampshire ready to collect my data. This was field biology, where you cannot control variables very easily. You do that with statistics back in the lab. However, you do need to think about what data to collect. Thankfully my supervisor in Hampshire directed my efforts. She told me to go and have a look at the pheasants for the first few days, make up some mini-hypotheses and, simply through observation, get a sense of whether I was right.

I loved it! I got the opportunity to drive around a Hampshire farm early in the morning, and late in the afternoon. I had the privilege of watching the lives of some beautiful birds, and I had the autonomy of developing hypotheses (admittedly under the big question from my supervisor).

I then moved to Sheffield, and undertook fieldwork on a rather wonderful little African bird – the red-billed buffalo weaver bird – from Namibia. I had complete autonomy. My supervisor kicked me off the back of our pick-up truck at some nests, with the words, 'I'll be back later – watch them, and see if you can work out what's going on.'

This wasn't the straitjacket of hypothesis, results and conclusion. This was thinking! This was an opportunity to think creatively, to make mistakes, to get puzzled. As John Dewey said, 'If you are made to think, then you'll learn.' And he was right. I learnt so much about that bird in four hours with a pair of binoculars. I really was 'working out' the bird's social system, I was 'messing around' with ideas and making hypotheses which I would then go on to test systematically over the next four years. It is this that makes Science wonderful. Of course, learning about scientific ideas is fascinating, and I owe a huge debt to inspirational school teachers and lecturers. But my first real experience of doing Science didn't come until the Hampshire pheasant fieldwork and the Namibian bush. That's why Science is important to me, and partly why I became a Science teacher: to bring that sense of being a scientist to children at a much earlier age.

# Why should students study Science?

So we've almost come full circle. Why should your students learn about Science? Because learning Science:

- ensures that students realise the importance of evidence in making decisions and coming to conclusions, not just about scientific issues, but about social and ethical issues too
- is about gaining understanding and skills that will allow students to work in scientific fields, earning a living and contributing to their country's economy
- is about developing the skills of observation, classification, interpretation and communication, which are useful beyond scientific endeavour, in everyday life
- is about students understanding their environment, and making the appropriate choices to help contribute to preserving our planet's resources and to ensure sustainable development, whichever country they live in
- is about unpicking arguments, seeking justification, having the courage to think creatively and look for solutions.

These skills are fundamental to scientists, but also fundamental to our everyday lives, and to the decision-making processes of governments the world over.

## Summary

- Learning about Science promotes systematic and critical thinking in your students, and involves learning content knowledge as well as skills.

- Becoming a scientist involves asking questions, generating hypotheses and undertaking practical work and inquiry.

- Doing Science involves thinking hard, being creative and 'playing around' with ideas.

- Studying Science gives your students important skills, allows them to unpick arguments and enables them to make reasoned and sensible choices.

# 4 | Key considerations

# What have I learnt through teaching Science?

Professional learning – what we learn while doing our jobs – is important to how we teach. We learn from our own experience, and that of others, and it's this type of learning that underpins our teaching practice day to day. So what are the three key things I have learnt that underpin my own Science teaching practice, and which are worth sharing with you?

## 1. Know what you're teaching

My own understanding of Science has never been better! If you're going to teach Science, you have to understand it. That doesn't mean reading from a textbook just before the lesson. First, you have to think about the fundamental ideas that lie behind what you are trying to teach. You then have to think about how to build up the ideas progressively, enabling students to learn step by step, until they eventually understand. Thinking through the lesson's storyline like this is essential, and it has done wonders for my own subject knowledge.

For example, when trying to teach osmosis, you would start with particle theory, move on to diffusion, think about different concentrations of solute and water, predict direction of diffusion of solute and water between different concentrations, and then predict what will happen across a partially-permeable membrane.

## 2. Use questions instead of giving information

Because we're teachers, we do sometimes teach too much. I certainly did. But then I realised that it's all very well telling students things, but could I avoid it and, by doing so, help students learn more effectively? The answer is yes. For example, I used to ask students to copy down sentences into their books. Instead, I swapped the sentences for questions. Students answered the questions, and wrote down exactly the same ideas, but they had been forced to think about those ideas. I made the same change when explaining ideas. Instead of telling them, I thought about questions in advance which could draw the ideas out of the students themselves. In fact, when I teach the whole class from the front of the room, I 'bounce' from one question to the other, building the developing explanation on the board. You may want to tailor your questions to the individuals. For example, you may ask one student **what** a particular organ is called, but you may ask a higher-achieving student **how** that organ works.

## 3. Get students to work out ideas for themselves

When I first started teaching, I already realised that explanations had to be well thought out and well structured, to give students a chance of understanding. But students don't learn just by **receiving** information. Even if you lecture a group of undergraduates, they are thinking about what you're saying, fitting it into what they already know, and building links between concepts. So when I'm planning a lesson, I think about what I want students to understand, and then I think about how students can work it out for themselves, and what I can give them to do which will make that happen. A really simple example would involve students collecting and plotting data to work out the relationship between two variables by themselves.

# What challenges does a teacher of Science have to overcome?

## 1. Teaching out of your specialism

We all know what it's like if you're teaching outside of your specialism. For me as a biologist, teaching Physics used to be a real challenge. But why was this?

Many of us feel like Biology teachers, Chemistry teachers or Physics teachers, who teach the other subjects reluctantly when we have to. When teaching out of specialism, we can feel like a fish out of water. We may also feel less secure about our subject knowledge, and we may simply be less well-practised.

There are also differences in the disciplines themselves, and how the curriculum is structured. Let's take an example. In Biology, we study the digestive system of the human body as part of human biology. We also study photosynthesis as part of green plants. But we don't often study nutrition as a big idea, with examples from humans and plants. But Physics does this. It teaches big ideas, such as waves, energy, electricity, and uses different contexts to exemplify them.

That's not all. In Biology, the specification contains 'nuggets' of knowledge, about, for example, the kidney. But in Physics, we don't teach 'facts' in the same way. Rather, we teach models or explanatory stories which are used to make sense of physical phenomena. Sometimes an explanation which helps us understand one idea can directly conflict with another. For example, I used to teach electric current as electrons carrying packets of charge, but when you try to explain why current splits equally in two branches of a parallel circuit, this explanation falls down.

This conflict used to confuse me, and because of that my students were also confused. It was only when I understood that Physics is made up of these explanatory stories, rather than the 'facts' of Biology, that I taught Physics more effectively.

## 2. Practical work

Science teachers know that practical work is important. It can help students to learn conceptual ideas, but also helps them learn the process skills of Science, and gives them experience 'as scientists'. But the resources required for practical work can be difficult to acquire, particularly in some countries, and the cost of them may be prohibitive. So how do you convince your head teacher that it's worth the effort?

Head teachers care about students' learning, so start there. Practicals can sometimes simply be a demonstration of some theoretical idea which you have already taught, so their 'added value' to students' learning is limited. Recent research by Ian Abrahams and Michael Reiss helps to make sure the practical work we use is effective. They identify two levels of effectiveness (see Figure 8.3 in Chapter 8 **Language awareness**). At level 1, a practical is effective if it enables students to do and see the things intended by the teacher. At level 2, a practical is effective if it enables students to learn the things intended by the teacher, whether they are process skills or conceptual learning. By thinking about practical work in this way, you can ensure that the practical work you do is adding value to students' learning, and justify its importance to your head teacher.

---

Teacher Tip

Sometimes when teaching out of specialism, our lack of experience can affect how safely we run our laboratory. For example, pushing a pipette into a pipette filler needs to be done safely (so that it doesn't snap and cause injury). But if you are a Physics or Biology teacher, you may not realise how to do it safely. Because of this, always draw on your technician's and your subject-specialist colleagues' experience in order to plan safe practical work.

---

# What special resources are required?

As any Science teacher knows, to teach Science effectively requires equipment and a practical laboratory. It is beyond the scope of this book to list all the equipment you need for such a laboratory, or to provide a specification for laboratory design. However, there are helpful resources available which do just that. In terms of design and outfitting of Science laboratories for schools, the Association for Science Education website (the professional body for Science teachers in the UK) provides industry standard guidance.

In terms of equipment and resources, there is considerable guidance available online for the resources needed in a Physics, Chemistry or Biology laboratory. However, much of this advice comes from commercial suppliers, and it's important not to over–spend according to their guidance. The variety of resources required will be related to the curriculum offered in schools. For example, Cambridge International Examinations provides guidance within its IGCSE® specification for equipment required in a Science laboratory, over and above standard lab equipment. They also publish a booklet entitled *Planning for Practical Science in School*.

---

Teacher Tip

When thinking about resourcing, make sure you are working with an experienced technician. A good technician is extremely valuable in terms of prior knowledge and understanding of what is needed to teach Science.

---

# What challenges might students face in studying Science?

## 1. Mathematical skill level

There is lots of evidence that students find it hard to apply their mathematical skills when learning Science. Changing the subject in an equation, scaling graphs and drawing lines of best fit can be a real challenge for students. How often have you found students taking a very long time to draw a graph which they would have drawn easily in a Maths lesson? So why do students find it so difficult to use Maths in Science?

- Students can learn Maths procedurally, which means they don't understand the fundamental Maths, and don't realise how to apply it to a real-life scientific problem.
- Scientific problems are not clearly 'signposted' from a mathematical point of view. In Maths, the problem is written in order for students to solve it. But in Science, a student must identify the Maths required, and then remember how to use it.
- Students are often asked to understand a scientific concept at the same time as carrying out the Maths required, which serves neither purpose effectively.
- Students may lack experience in implementing the Maths skills required.
- Students may lack confidence in their mathematical ability, or simply be very uninterested in Maths.

Because of this, it is important to help students identify the Maths skills required, to recap how to use them, and to help them apply their Maths to the scientific context. Being explicit about when Maths is needed is important, while providing reassurance and enthusiasm.

---

Teacher Tip

Make a list of Mathematics skills needed to teach your subject. For each, make brief notes about how to support students' use of each skill. There is some helpful guidance available from the Association for Science Education in the UK.

---

## 2. Language level

Scientific language can make Science appear difficult. Difficult terminology can act as a barrier to students' learning. Some everyday words can have very different meanings in Science. For example, energy, work and power mean one thing in Science lessons and something else in everyday life. But students can also have difficulty using normal English words in a Science context. Cassels and Johnstone in 1985 found students had difficulty understanding and using words such as abundant, linear and random. Because of this, we should realise that learning Science is like learning a new language, and help learners accordingly (see Chapter 9 **Language awareness**).

# What challenges might students face when being assessed in Science?

For any student, understanding examination questions can be difficult. For students working with English as a second language, they can present an even greater challenge. To help them, try to focus on the command words from examination questions. Many of these may be strongly related to the processes of Science, such as analyse, compare, calculate and evaluate. Helping students understand what is required of them is essential if they are to demonstrate their scientific understanding.

---

**Teacher Tip**

Make a booklet that lists examination command words and their definitions for your students.

---

**Summary**

- Know what you're teaching; use questions to draw ideas out of students, and make students learn by working out ideas for themselves.

- Good Science teaching and learning need practical resources.

- Students face challenges in using Maths in Science lessons, and with the language of Science.

- Students need to understand the command words in Science examinations.

# 5 | Interpreting a syllabus

# What to look for in a syllabus

Having downloaded your syllabus, take some time to read it through. It's tempting to go straight to the part which tells you what students must know and understand. But in many cases, this carries only 50% of the marks. Look for the following:

- **Aims.** These are frequently forgotten, but they are important to examiners when setting examination papers. The more you understand them and try to think about them when planning your course, the better you will prepare your students.
- **Learning objectives.** You will find these in the knowledge and understanding section. You will probably see this section as your main priority. Sometimes it is broken down into useful modules, which can form the basis of units of teaching. In other cases, it is broken down into sections which reflect academic links between topics. Do not assume you can teach the content in the order provided. Even if examiners have tried to structure it in an order to help conceptual development, the order may not necessarily work for you and your students.
- **Assessment objectives.** Although you probably think that the objectives of assessment are to assess the learning objectives, this is only one third of the story. In many Science syllabuses, the assessment objectives include:

  1 Knowledge with understanding
  2 Handling information and problem solving
  3 Experimental skills and investigations

  This makes sense, as the three of them together are what we hold important in educating new scientists.

- **Type and nature of assessment.** You need to know what the assessment weighting is between the assessment objectives. Knowledge with understanding is often worth about 50% of the marks, while the other assessment objectives may be worth about 25% each. This comes as a surprise to many teachers, who fail to prepare their students effectively. You also need to look at how assessment actually happens. For example, experimental skills and investigations may be assessed primarily through coursework, while handling information may be partly assessed through coursework and partly through examination. Reading examiners' reports (available from examination board websites) can help you to see where students have been poorly prepared.

---

Teacher Tip

Make sure you're working with the correct syllabus. A single examination board may produce syllabuses for Combined Science, Double Science, Triple Science, Biology, Chemistry and Physics. Ask your head of department to give you the syllabus number. Check the date on the front, too. It should say something like 'For examination in June…', followed by the year. This is very important, as examination boards review and update their syllabuses regularly.

---

# Structuring and scaffolding learning

## Think long term

Students should learn more fundamental concepts early on, and progress to more complex, sophisticated ones later. Their learning should build upon what they have already learnt (progression), and make links to different conceptual areas (continuity). Using a mind map can help you to think this through:

1   Look at the learning objectives and identify the key concepts being taught. Looking at the section headings in the syllabus is sometimes quite helpful. Write these down on a large sheet of paper. Remember: try to see beyond the learning objectives themselves to identify the key ideas underpinning them.
2   Draw arrows between the concepts. For example, if you need to know A before you can learn B, draw an arrow from A to B. Once you've finished, you should be able to see some patterns. Concepts that have a lot of arrows pointing towards them should appear later in the course. Those that primarily have arrows pointing away from them will appear earlier in the course.

3  Now add lines between the concepts that are somehow related. For example, digestion and breathing are related, as they provide the raw materials for respiration. You should see clustering of concepts. This clustering, and the arrows in point 2, should give you a good idea of how to divide the course into units. You may find the examiner who wrote the syllabus has done a pretty good job of this already. You may also have a long-term plan you've used before, or examples you can download from the examination board. But it is important to think it through yourself.

# Think medium term

Take each unit in turn. Write down the key ideas covered, and what students need to know already before they begin. Add the learning objectives from the syllabus. Look for opportunities here to cover objectives within handling information and problem solving, and experimental skills and investigations. Ask yourself in what order the ideas need to be to give the unit good progression. Split the learning objectives into blocks which build upon each other.

For each block, give recommendations for teaching and learning approaches, and identify opportunities for assessment, to assess both prior knowledge and learning after teaching.

- **Assessing prior knowledge and dealing with misconceptions.** For each block, ask yourself what students need to know first, and what their common misconceptions are likely to be. Think about how you'll find out what they know, and how you'll help them to overcome their misconceptions (see Chapter 6 **Active learning** and Chapter 7 **Assessment for Learning**).
- **Developing learning activities.** Express the learning objectives from each block as outcomes. You can think of these as 'what will students be able to do if they understand this learning objective'? Use the outcomes to help you suggest learning activities and follow–up homework (see Chapter 6 **Active learning**).
- **Assessment.** Think about how to find out if students have learnt (see Chapter 7 **Assessment for Learning**). Try to build learning activities that provide assessment information, as well as helping students to learn, or allowing you to undertake formative assessment.

# 5

## Approaches to learning and teaching Science

Don't restrict yourself to knowledge and understanding, but also think about students' skills in handling information and problem solving, and experimental skills and investigations. It's not enough to provide opportunities to do these things. Your scheme of work should also make clear how you expect students to learn them.

## Pacing

Now that you've divided the syllabus into units, and the units into sets of learning objectives, allocate time to both. The amount of time available is seldom under your control, but think about:

*   How many lessons each week?
*   How long are the lessons?
*   How long is the course?

---

### Teacher Tip

Your syllabus or examination board will recommend how many guided learning hours should be provided for the qualification you are teaching.

---

You can see an example of a long-term plan for Biology IGCSE in Table 5.1.

| Term 1 | Term 2 | Term 3 | Term 4 | Term 5 | Term 6 |
|---|---|---|---|---|---|
| Characteristics of living things | Human nutrition | Plant nutrition | Diseases and immunity | Reproduction | Biotechnology and genetic engineering |
| Cells, tissues and organs | | | | | |
| Diffusion, osmosis and active transport | Gas exchange | Transport in plants | Excretion, coordination and response | Inheritance, cell division, variation and selection | Human influences on ecosystems |
| Biological molecules and enzymes | Respiration | Transport in animals | Drugs and health | Food chains and ecosystems | *Practice for written examination* |

**Table 5.1:** Exemplar long-term plan.

Look at Table 5.1 and try to think about the fundamental concepts introduced in each unit, then think how they are revisited and built upon later in the course. Identify any changes you may want to make to the plan.

For each unit, look at the way in which you've divided the learning objectives and the skills you've pencilled in alongside. Think about how long each of those will take, and allocate objectives and learning activities to each lesson appropriately. It's useful to present a single lesson on a single page of your scheme of work. Although there are no firm rules, you may want to include the following:

- learning objectives
- learning outcomes
- assessment strategies
- differentiation and inclusion strategies
- suggested learning activities
- lesson timings
- syllabus references
- resources required
- homework
- links to other units and other subjects
- technician notes.

## Teacher Tip

You may find a scheme of work for your syllabus available for download online, often uploaded by other teachers around the world. It is almost certain that you will need to amend one of these to make it work in your school, but a downloaded scheme of work can be really helpful in devising your own scheme of work.

## Summary

- Make sure you read your syllabus so you know the aims, learning objectives, assessment objectives and type and nature of assessment.

- Plan your programme of study so that it shows progression. Don't forget to include handling information, problem solving, experimental skills and investigations.

- Divide the programme of study into units and lessons, plan the learning activities and allocate the available time. Don't forget to build in opportunities to assess students' learning.

# 6

# Active learning

# What is active learning?

Active learning is a pedagogical practice that places student learning at its centre. It focuses on *how* students learn, not just on *what* they learn. We as teachers need to encourage students to 'think hard', rather than passively receive information. Active learning encourages students to take responsibility for their learning and supports them in becoming independent and confident learners in school and beyond.

Research shows us that it is not possible to transmit understanding to students by simply telling them what they need to know. Instead, we need to make sure that we challenge students' thinking and support them in building their own understanding. Active learning encourages more complex thought processes, such as evaluating, analysing and synthesising, which foster a greater number of neural connections in the brain. While some students may be able to create their own meaning from information received passively, others will not. Active learning enables all students to build knowledge and understanding in response to the opportunities we provide.

# Why adopt an active learning approach?

We can enrich all areas of the curriculum, at all stages, by embedding an active learning approach.

In active learning, we need to think not only about the content but also about the process. It gives students greater involvement and control over their learning. This encourages all students to stay focused on their learning, which will often give them greater enthusiasm for their studies. Active learning is intellectually stimulating and taking this approach encourages a level of academic discussion with our students that we, as teachers, can also enjoy. Healthy discussion means that students are engaging with us as a partner in their learning.

Students will better be able to revise for examinations in the sense that revision really is 're-vision' of the ideas that they already understand.

Active learning develops students' analytical skills, supporting them to be better problem solvers and more effective in their application of knowledge. They will be prepared to deal with challenging and unexpected situations. As a result, students are more confident in continuing to learn once they have left school and are better equipped for the transition to higher education and the workplace.

# What are the challenges of incorporating active learning?

When people start thinking about putting active learning into practice, they often make the mistake of thinking more about the activity they want to design than about the learning. The most important thing is to put the student and the learning at the centre of our planning. A task can be quite simple but still get the student to think critically and independently. Sometimes a complicated task does not actually help to develop the students' thinking or understanding at all. We need to consider carefully what we want our students to learn or understand and then shape the task to activate this learning.

# Active learning in Science

Active learning is not a new thing in Science. In fact, Science itself is an active process, which builds knowledge in a similar way to how ideas are built in your classroom. John Dewey said: 'Give the pupils something to do, not something to [rote] learn, and if the doing is of such a nature as to demand thinking, learning naturally results.' By generating that thinking, students take ownership of their learning, and they are more motivated to learn.

# Start from students' prior ideas

If learning is going to mean anything to students, it needs to build on what they know and understand already. Our students have spent their childhood trying to make sense of the world, and they develop their own scientific theories as a result. However, sometimes these theories can be wrong. They tend to be built upon everyday experiences, and may prevent a student from learning what we want to teach. Sometimes they are linked to specialist language. For example, weight means something different in Science to everyday life. Can we ignore these ideas? No – if we don't deal with them, they can slow down further conceptual development.

If you want students to change their ideas, you need to make them realise that their ideas are wrong, by generating conflict in their mind between their own ideas and the evidence.

How can you make this work? Ask students to make predictions before a piece of practical work. Their prediction is based on their prior ideas, but the data they collect may conflict with those ideas. You can do the same with simulations: ask students to make predictions, run the simulation, and generate that conflict in their minds. Whatever you do, remember that if students see that conflict, they will be more open to taking on the new ideas.

---

Teacher Tip

As you get more experienced, you will know many of the misconceptions which students tend to hold about scientific ideas, and you can attempt to challenge them accordingly. You will find many lists of common misconceptions by doing an internet search for 'Science misconceptions'.

---

# Working out ideas for themselves

However, it's not enough just to break down students' 'wrong ideas'. You have to help them build the correct understanding of a concept. And that means getting students to work out the correct ideas for themselves.

---

## ☑ LESSON IDEA ONLINE 6.1: TWEET YOUR MISCONCEPTIONS

In pairs, on paper, students answer a question designed to uncover their misconceptions; they must use fewer than 140 characters. They pass the tweet between groups, where it is refined and revised before being returned to the original pair. They then decide what questions they want to ask the teacher.

---

## LESSON IDEA 6.2: USING MISCONCEPTIONS

Use students' misconceptions as the platform for learning. Put their different ideas on the board, and ask students to say which ones they agree with. Ask students to justify their ideas, and to explain to other students why the misconceptions are 'wrong'. Invite students to add ideas to each other's explanations, until most of the class have adopted the correct ideas.

To help students understand concepts, you need to get the storyline right. Break down the storyline into steps, and think about how to get students to work out each step for themselves. Think about which ideas need to come first, and which ideas build on the first one.

Having reached this point, you can start to think about what kinds of lesson activities will help students to build up their ideas effectively. It's easy to simply choose activities 'off the shelf' from your departmental collection of resources, or from the internet. However, when you find a resource on the internet, or when you're trying to invent a resource for students to learn from, think about the following criteria:

- Does it allow students to start with something familiar? This may be conceptual knowledge which they already have, but could also just be a familiar context from everyday life, within which you set the learning.
- Does it allow students to work out ideas for themselves? If it's a worksheet, look at the questions. Do they simply find out what students know (you'll see questions starting with 'What?', 'State', or 'List'), or do they prompt students to think (questions like 'Why?' or 'How?')? Does the answer to one question help them to answer the next question? Does each step of the learning activity help them to 'work out' one step in the storyline of the lesson?
- Does it start easy, to give students confidence that they can 'do it', and then ask them to think more deeply?
- Does it both help students to learn and elicit evidence of learning?
- Does it allow you, or other students, to support each student's learning?
- Does it build on students' personal interests, and allow them to feel that they are pursuing their own goals? You may want to give them a choice of learning activity, or tie the learning activity to their interests.

Different activities lend themselves to being completed individually, in pairs, in groups or all of these. Building ideas together can be much more effective than building ideas alone. This is because students can help each other 'in their own words', but also because it makes students feel responsible for their learning, because they have an obligation to each other.

---

Teacher Tip

To encourage you to really think about the criteria above, use them to help you develop a worksheet for one of your lessons.

---

# Group work

So many of us find group work difficult to manage. Why? Because we worry students that will go 'off-topic' and lose their focus on scientific learning. To help group work happen successfully, think about the following:

- **Make each group fit for purpose.** Who is in each group? What does the group need to do? What kinds of skills do you need in each group? What kinds of ideas are you trying to get each group to build? What difficulties may students encounter? What activity should you use to build the ideas? You don't have to ask these questions in this order. If you design groups according to the concept you are trying to build, you may ask the questions in a different order entirely.
- **What does each group member do?** It's important to work out what role each group member should take because it gives students purpose. If you don't allocate roles, some students may lose interest, sit back and learn nothing. If you ensure everyone participates, this can give everyone the chance to say what they think, have it challenged by others in the group and rebuild their understanding.
- **What is the outcome required?** Make sure each group is working towards a definite outcome. Without an outcome, students won't be focused. Outcomes will depend on the task; they may be shared or joint. Give students an explicit time limit to work towards to maintain the pace of the lesson.

# Making thinking happen

Thinking doesn't 'just happen' among groups of students. In fact, it may not happen at all! Thinking depends on the questions you ask. Think about what you want students to think about, and choose your command words appropriately. Bloom's Taxonomy (see Table 6.1) is quite helpful to make you choose the questions to match your purpose, or choose learning activities themselves.

| Remember | Draw, Identify, Locate, Label, Select, Write, Outline, List, Name, State, Record, Repeat, Tell, Investigate, Define, Memorise, Recite |
| --- | --- |
| Comprehend | Explain, Confirm, Infer, Convert, Describe, Paraphrase, Estimate, Predict, Match, Discuss, Summarise, Defend, Interpret, Express, Change, Voice-over |
| Apply | Apply, Modify, Build, Construct, Solve, Report, Sketch, Produce, Use, Make, Draw, Choose |
| Analyse | Analyse, Sort, Differentiate between, Examine, Compare, Categorise, Classify, Distinguish, Subdivide, Contrast, Rank |
| Synthesise | Combine, Generate, Design, Plan, Devise, Hypothesise, Revise, Compose, What if?, Organise, Develop, Create, Rearrange, Predict, Improve |
| Evaluate | Critique, Criticise, Appraise, Assess, Conclude, Justify, Judge, Rate, Decide, Consider, Relate, Recommend |

**Table 6.1:** Making thinking happen through choosing the correct command word.

Each item in the following list could form the basis for a learning activity in a Science classroom. By using different command words with an activity, you can give it a different purpose in helping students to learn. For example, you could have '**explain** an animation', '**design** an animation' or '**voice-over** an animation'.

story, letter, blog, news report, website, cartoon strip, voice-over, advertisement, flicker book, graphic organiser (like a concept cartoon, KWL grid or flowchart), machine, board game, model, storyboard, animation, video, set of instructions, consequence map, role play, imaginary organism, information leaflet, piece of persuasive writing, mark scheme for an exam paper, crossword, wordsearch, fill-in-the-blanks, unfinished sentences, unfinished story, unlabelled diagram, jigsaw, list of key words, questions, brainstorm, debate, discuss, concept cartoon, model, answers, similarities, differences, advantages, disadvantages, diagram, paragraph, drawing, graph, other students' work, script

---

### LESSON IDEA 6.3: APPLYING COMMAND WORDS

Take two of the activity ideas which look relevant to a lesson you are planning. Find four different command words for each, which would give each activity a different purpose in helping students to learn in your classroom. Include one of these activities in your lesson planning.

---

# Facilitating active learning

So you've got a classroom in which everyone is learning, everyone is taking responsibility for their learning, and students are working independently and together to build their own understanding. But when all this is happening, what do **you** do? You're not teaching from the front, so it can be difficult to understand what your role is. Try to follow the guidance below:

- Pose questions instead of giving answers. Try not to answer students' questions directly. Ask them a question in return, to help them think up their own answers.
- Build relationships with your students by listening, encouraging, being interested in what they are doing and asking them questions about what they are doing. Create a supportive and inspiring classroom environment! If you have a good relationship, they will work for you, rather than against you.
- Try to circulate around the class, look at students' work, and listen to their conversations to get a picture of how everyone is doing and what common problems they're having. Deal with those problems 'as a class'.
- Help students to manage their space. When you create learning activities, they can be resource heavy. If students' tables or laboratory benches are untidy, students won't be able to focus on what you've

asked them to do. Help them to manage their space so they can focus on the task.

- Give value to students' work, either by praising it explicitly and displaying it on the wall, or by using it as part of your own teaching. Students need to feel they are good at Science to have confidence to learn it.
- Help students to realise they can make mistakes and it is OK to find things difficult. Value mistakes, mention them explicitly and use them to build the next steps in the storyline of the lesson. Encourage them to take risks and explore a line of thought, even if it eventually goes nowhere. Getting 'stuck and unstuck' is an important part of the learning process. Offer students just enough help to get them back on track, or simply wait for them to puzzle it out for themselves.
- Help your students to keep trying when they find things hard. You can give a few hints, ask questions to make them think in a different way or encourage them to think of a different solution. You should try to offer 'just enough' to help them overcome their obstacles.
- Encourage students to think about what they are learning. For example, if you see a wrong answer on their page, ask them to explain their thinking.
- Be observant and try to find out what everyone is doing so that you are ready to respond to different individual responses and needs.
- Encourage collaboration with other students. If students seek support from each other, it gives you more time to support those who really need the help. Some teachers have a rule that says: 'Ask at least two other students, and then you can ask me.' Get rid of the concept of 'cheating' – students should become learning resources for each other.

---

**Teacher Tip**

Try to avoid the temptation to teach too much. There's value in allowing students to puzzle it out for themselves. Your aim is for them to explore and develop their own understanding. You may need to sit on your hands to stop yourself intervening too often!

---

# Learning through inquiry

So far, we've talked about starting from the students' starting points, designing a storyline that shows progression (builds upon what goes before), and getting students to work ideas out for themselves, either individually or in groups. When we design learning activities, we're usually thinking about learning outcomes from the syllabus. However, imagine a case where students are helped to set their own learning objectives, to decide their own learning activities and to come to their own conclusions! This is perhaps several steps too far for many of us (and may not fit the syllabus very well), but giving students the chance to do inquiry, and to learn Science through the process of inquiry, is a fantastic aspiration.

If you do decide to use inquiry, it doesn't have to be this 'open' route; often more structure would help students to learn more effectively. Look at Table 6.2 to help you think about how to design inquiry in your lessons, and how 'student-directed' to make it.

## Teacher Tip

You don't need to be in the same column of Table 6.2 for everything. For example, **you** may give students a question to investigate, but then get **them** to plan what data to collect.

|  | 1 (Open) | 2 (Guided) | 3 (Structured) |
|---|---|---|---|
| **Question** | Students decide what to investigate. | Students choose what to investigate from a list given by the teacher. | The teacher gives the students a single question to investigate. |
| **Evidence** | Students think about what evidence to collect, and they collect it. | The teacher gives students a choice of what data to collect, or what pre-provided data to use. | Students are given evidence/ data by the teacher. |

| | 1 (Open) | 2 (Guided) | 3 (Structured) |
|---|---|---|---|
| **Analyse** | Students decide how to analyse evidence. | The teacher suggests ways in which students may analyse their evidence, which they choose between. | Students are told how to analyse their evidence. |
| **Explain** | Students create their own explanation of the evidence. | The teacher suggests some ways to formulate an explanation, which students choose between. | Students are given a way to formulate an explanation based on evidence. |
| **Connect** | Students link their explanation to scientific knowledge, researching that knowledge themselves from other resources. | Students are directed to other resources, and shown how to form links to scientific knowledge. | Students are given other resources and shown the links with scientific knowledge. |
| **Communicate** | Students choose how to communicate and justify explanations. | Students are given broad guidelines on how to justify and communicate explanations. | Students are given all the steps to justify and communicate explanations by the teacher. |
| **Reflect** | Students decide how to reflect on and evaluate the inquiry and what they've learnt from it. | Students are given broad guidelines for reflecting on and evaluating the inquiry and what they've learnt from it. | Students are given a structured framework for reflecting on and evaluating the inquiry and what they've learnt from it. |

**Table 6.2:** Structuring learning through inquiry.

If you ensure that students are investigating a question that is relevant to the intended learning (see Chapter 8 **Metacognition**), the students can build their learning themselves through the inquiry; at the same time they will build their inquiry skills (which are also a very significant part of the syllabus!).

**Teacher Tip**

You will find that people define inquiry in different ways. Because of this, some people will say it is wonderful for teaching and learning, and others will say it is terrible. This difference is usually because they haven't thought about the difference between Open, Guided and Structured inquiry. Use Table 6.2 to help you implement inquiry effectively, and reflect upon your success.

**Summary**

• Students learn actively in Science if they are made to think. Thinking together in groups can be very helpful.

• Start from students' prior ideas, and help them to build their learning, rather than simply telling them the ideas. Think carefully about what you want them to learn, what they'll be able to do when they've learnt it and how to design or choose an activity to achieve that.

• Facilitate the learning process effectively: make students feel confident, make students think and avoid the temptation to give them all the answers.

• Use inquiry to help students learn, and provide enough structure to help them complete the inquiry, but not so much that they don't think for themselves.

In the remainder of this book, you will think about active learning in Science from a number of different perspectives, and you will be introduced to a broad range of activities to help achieve it.

# Assessment for Learning

7

# What is Assessment for Learning?

Assessment for Learning (AfL) is a teaching approach that generates feedback that can be used to improve students' performance. Students become more involved in the learning process and, from this, gain confidence in what they are expected to learn and to what standard. We as teachers gain insights into a student's level of understanding of a particular concept or topic, which helps to inform how we support their progression.

We need to understand the meaning and method of giving purposeful feedback to optimise learning. Feedback can be informal, such as oral comments to help students think through problems, or formal, such as the use of rubrics to help clarify and scaffold learning and assessment objectives.

# Why use Assessment for Learning?

By following well-designed approaches to AfL, we can understand better how our students are learning and use this to plan what we will do next with a class or individual students (see Figure 7.1). We can help our students to see what they are aiming for and to understand what they need to do to get there. AfL makes learning visible; it helps students understand more accurately the nature of the material they are learning and themselves as learners. The quality of interactions and feedback between students and teachers becomes critical to the learning process.

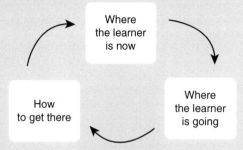

**Figure 7.1:** How can we use this plan to help our students?

We can use AfL to help our students focus on specific elements of their learning and to take greater responsibility for how they might move forward. AfL creates a valuable connection between assessment and learning activities, as the clarification of objectives will have a direct impact on how we devise teaching and learning strategies. AfL techniques can support students in becoming more confident in what they are learning, reflective in how they are learning, more likely to try out new approaches, and more engaged in what they are being asked to learn.

# What are the challenges of incorporating AfL?

The use of AfL does not mean that we need to test students more frequently. It would be easy to just increase the amount of summative assessment and use this formatively as a regular method of helping us decide what to do next in our teaching. We can judge how much learning has taken place through ways other than testing, including, above all, communicating with our students in a variety of ways and getting to know them better as individuals.

# What does success 'look' like?

The courses we teach are often given to us as a list of statements or facts. The first step to successful AfL is to be very clear about what success 'looks' like, and this isn't just about answering exam questions. What is it that the students could say or do at the end of the lesson to show us that they have really understood? If you wanted to know if a student understood chemical bonding then you could give them a periodic table and some chemical formulae and ask the student to sort them into piles of ionic and covalently bonded molecules, even adding compounds that the student had never seen. Or when studying adaptations in animals, you could ask for possible reasons for characteristics in an invented animal.

Success doesn't always have to be shown by answering a question. It might be that you give students some practical equipment and ask them to complete a task that they must explain – for example, balancing an object to show an understanding of centre of mass, or putting a mark on the floor where they think a projectile will land. It is critical to be clear about how students can show success, so that we can decide the best way to get them there and how to help along the way.

## ☑ LESSON IDEA ONLINE 7.1: EXIT TICKET

For any lesson you are about to teach, think of one question that you feel is the best way to assess if the lesson has been successful. Just before the end of the lesson, ask the class to write their answers on a postcard and give it to you on the way out as an 'exit ticket'. A quick look through afterwards will tell you how successful the lesson really was and might suggest where to start the next lesson!

# Finding a starting point

Every day, students see Science in action and develop ideas about how the world works. Unfortunately, not all of these are right. The sun looks as though it **does** go around the Earth, blood in our veins looks as though it is blue and when sugar is put into warm water it really does seem to disappear. One of the key messages when thinking about AfL is to consider what the students already know before we can move them forward. We need to start where they are.

It's difficult to ask each student individually, so we need to be clear about the critical key ideas in any lesson and find quick and efficient ways to find out what the class already know about them. Knowing how to spell 'sodium', and that it is an element, are both parts of learning chemistry, but if a student does not know what an element is, then this is likely to cause more problems in class than a spelling error. As teachers, we need to think about what knowledge or understanding will be a barrier to what comes next and try to address this before we move on.

Teacher Tip

*Science Formative Assessment* by Page Keeley has many Science AfL ideas and examples to use and adapt with free resources on the site.

## LESSON IDEA 7.2: ASSESSING PRIOR KNOWLEDGE
Look over a recent lesson and write down all the facts and ideas that the students were expected to know already. From this list, decide on the two or three most important ones and then come up with questions or activities that you could do in the first five minutes of a lesson to check if the students really did know them.

# How to find out what the students know

We could start lessons with a short test or quiz and that can work well; however, there are other, more engaging and equally valid ways to elicit what the students know. If you were starting a new topic, one way to begin would be to research some of the common misconceptions that students have about that topic. Then you could create a list of ten statements about that topic, some correct and some based on these misconceptions. You could give these to the class and ask them to sort them into piles labelled **TRUE**, **FALSE** and **NOT SURE**, explaining their reasons to each other.

Some example statements from the topic of forces might be:

- When you go into space or on the Moon, gravity disappears.
- Friction always acts in the opposite direction to motion.
- Weight and mass are the same quantity.
- Objects need a force to change direction.
- Moving objects need a force to keep them moving.

## LESSON IDEA 7.3: SECONDARY RESEARCH

For a topic that you will be teaching soon, research some of the most common misconceptions that students have. Use this to plan a student-led discussion activity that allows students to explore their existing understanding of a topic before the main activities. *Making Sense of Secondary Science* by Driver, Squires, Rushworth and Wood-Robinson (1994) is an excellent resource listing common misconceptions.

This task makes students explain their ideas to their peers. They can feel less embarrassed about being wrong when talking to their peers and so this helps to create a classroom environment where students feel able to say what they know and what they are struggling with. If we build a supportive classroom environment where students can discuss, share and challenge ideas without feeling judged, then we can help them become more confident, reflective, innovative and engaged. Getting the right atmosphere in class can be critical to the success of AfL and so it is worth the time and effort to get it right.

# Eliciting understanding and generating discussion

Some teachers use mini–whiteboards to get answers from all students and some have a 'no hands up' policy. Some write the name of each student on a lolly stick and then pick one at random to select who answers. These ways of asking questions aim to keep everyone engaged, as all students know they might be asked; these strategies can also stop a few keen students from dominating.

AfL is not just for the start and end of lessons – it should be going on all the time. Generating dialogue between students helps them challenge and test what they know, moving their learning forward. Table 7.1 lists techniques commonly used in Science to elicit understanding and generate discussion. Try to include some of these ideas in your lessons.

| Classroom technique | Notes |
|---|---|
| Wait time | Introduce a pause of a few seconds between asking a question and requesting a response, giving all students time to think. |
| Think, pair, share | After being asked a question, students think about their answer on their own, then discuss with another student and then share with a larger group. |
| Confidence score | As well as responding to a question, students say how confident they are, which encourages self-reflection. |
| Hot seat questioning | Several questions are shared around the class. Students answer these, and then follow-up questions can be randomly given to someone else (who moves into the 'hot seat'). The chance of being picked keeps everyone's attention. |
| One question, 30 answers | Using mini-whiteboards, student voting systems or simple A/B/C/D cards (for multiple choice questions), the teacher asks a question and the whole class respond. |
| Discussion questions | Pick questions without easy answers, requiring students to talk to each other about their ideas. |

**Table 7.1:** Techniques to elicit understanding and generate discussion.

# 7

---

Teacher Tip

Each day for a week, try out one or more of the ideas in Table 7.1 in a lesson. Ask a colleague to do the same and at the end of the week compare experiences.

---

There are times when, as a teacher, you need to lead the class, but it can be just as valuable to use the well-researched power of collaborative and cooperative learning to get students to help each other. It can be hard to hand over responsibility for the lesson to the class, but properly structured peer work can help all students develop their learning, confidence and self-reliance, as well as giving you time to focus on the students that need the most help. For cooperative work to be successful, goals need to be clear and individuals need to be accountable, so you should make sure you consider these when you are planning.

## ▣ LESSON IDEA ONLINE 7.4: ROLES, TEAMWORK AND PRACTICAL WORK

Take the instructions from a Science practical experiment and change them to allocate different roles for different students. For each role, write a job description, as well as one for the whole group, so that students have a common goal.

Other peer-work techniques are shown in Table 7.2.

| Peer-work technique | Notes |
|---|---|
| Peer marking | Share and explain a mark scheme to the class and get them to use it to mark each other's work. |
| Two stars and a wish | When marking each other's work, students list two good things about it (stars) and one way that they could make it better (wish). |
| Ask teacher last | Tell students that you'll only help if they have asked at least two of the class for help before coming to you. |
| Pre-flight checklist | Useful for work that has multiple requirements such as an experimental write-up. Using a list of requirements or expectations, students check each other's work and record what parts are included or missing. |

**Table 7.2:** Peer-work techniques.

# Responsive teaching

In any lesson, there are points where we think: '*Can I move on or do I need to go through this idea again?*' This decision is important when what comes next depends upon students understanding what has already been covered, otherwise they may get confused. This point is sometimes known as a **hinge-point**. A good question can help us decide whether we can move on or whether we need to go back and cover the material again in a different way. A good hinge-point question is one:

- that is quick to answer
- where it is easy to see everyone's response (e.g. multiple choice)
- where it's hard to get the right answer for the wrong reason
- that has answers based around common misconceptions.

An example using the topic of digestion might look like this:

## What/which statement(s) is/are correct?
**A**   Digestion begins when food enters the stomach.
**B**   The liver produces acid to help digestion.
**C**   Liquids we drink go straight from the stomach to the bladder.
**D**   Bacteria and enzymes help us break down food.

---

### Teacher Tip

Look over a set of lesson plans. For each lesson decide where the hinge-points are and, in each case, write a question or short activity that you could add into the lesson.

---

If everyone is right, we know we can move on, and if not, we can try a different approach. These questions help us plan to respond to student answers, particularly if not everyone knows the answer. We might then ask students to discuss their answers with each other, create multiple activities that they pick depending on their answer or come up with something else. Whether students are right or wrong, we should look for ways to challenge and develop their thinking. We cannot fill our lessons with multiple hinge-points, but using the right questions at the right time and planning what to do next will help us to support the whole class, not leaving anyone behind.

---

**LESSON IDEA 7.5: HINGE-POINT QUESTIONS**
Rewrite a lesson plan with one or two hinge-point questions added in. Plan multiple activities after each question depending on whether some, all or only a few of the class get the right answer.

---

# Asking useful questions

As teachers, we ask questions all day, perhaps not considering exactly why we are asking them. The response from Dylan Wiliam in his book *Embedded Formative Assessment* (2011) provides an excellent starting point:

> *'I suggest there are only two good reasons to ask questions in class: to cause thinking and to provide information for the teacher about what to do next.'*

Good questions need planning in advance. Having looked at the ways we can ask questions, we will now look at the types of questions we could ask.

Many questions asked in lessons are closed questions with a one- or two-word answer rather than open questions that require more thought. As well as using more open questions, we can use frameworks to help us consider good and challenging questions. Socratic questioning is one example, suggesting six question types.

- **Clarification:** to think about ideas *(e.g. Can you give me an example?)*
- **Assumptions:** to check the foundation thinking *(e.g. Will this always happen?)*
- **Evidence:** to justify thinking *(e.g. Why do you think this happens?)*
- **Alternatives:** to consider alternative viewpoints *(e.g. How else might you explain this?)*
- **Implication:** to consider consequences *(e.g. How does ...affect ... ?)*
- **Question the question:** to reflect on the questioning process itself *(e.g. Why might that question help?)*

## LESSON IDEA 7.6: CHOOSING 'GOOD' QUESTIONS

Pick a lesson that is coming up soon and, using the six question types, come up with a list of 'good' questions, together with what you think the 'good' answers are.

It is fine to use a different framework and you don't need to use all six question types. What matters is that we choose questions that make students think, and we should consider how to respond depending upon the answers they give.

## ⊡ LESSON IDEA ONLINE 7.7: WATCH THE DEMONSTRATION, ASK GOOD QUESTIONS

A demonstration can provide a great opportunity to practise and develop the questioning techniques of students.

Teacher Tip

Video or audio record one of your lessons, reviewing it with a focus just on the questions. Write them down and use the ideas here to classify them. Consider how you could improve them or what else you could have asked. It can be uncomfortable to relive our own lessons, but it can be a valuable activity.

# Providing effective feedback

Feedback is only powerful if students engage with it and are made to **think**. If we find out what they know and if we understand what success looks like, our feedback needs to guide them between the two. Ticks and crosses don't need action and so are easily ignored, while comments on how good/bad something is can get emotional responses which aren't helpful. Some feedback techniques are listed in Table 7.3.

| Technique | Notes/Examples |
|---|---|
| Allow time for a response | To make students value feedback, we must allow time for a response, perhaps at the start of a lesson. |
| Don't always be specific | Use feedback to support skills and learning more widely, rather than focusing on a single 'correct' response. For example, rather than writing something like 'Where is hydrogen formed?', you might write: 'When describing electrolysis, always consider the ions present, their charges and the charges of the anode and cathode to work out what might be produced and where.' |
| Turn feedback into a job | Make it clear that a response is expected. A comment like 'Four of these chemical equations are not balanced: which ones?' gives students a job to do. |
| Make it so students have to engage with it | You could write all the feedback for the whole class on a single sheet and get students to work out which comments apply to them. |
| Comments, not grades | Grades can be easily ignored. Try comment-only feedback. |

**Table 7.3:** Feedback techniques.

Effective feedback needs to be realistic and targeted and guide a student forwards. It will only work if the student responds to it, so we need to consider both what feedback we give and what we expect to happen next.

## Summary

Questions lie at the heart of good AfL. Here are four questions for you to consider to help you build better AfL into your lessons:

- Why are you asking the question? To assess learning, at a hinge-point, to promote discussion, or for something else? The reason may change what you ask and how.

- What is the best question to ask? Think about the questions before the lesson.

- How will you ask the question? Do you want answers from individuals or everyone? How you do this affects the classroom atmosphere.

- What will you do with the answer? Plan for the most likely answers.

# Metacognition

8

# What is metacognition?

Metacognition describes the processes involved when students plan, monitor, evaluate and make changes to their own learning behaviours. These processes help students to think about their own learning more explicitly and ensure that they are able to meet a learning goal that they have identified themselves or that we, as teachers, have set.

Metacognitive learners recognise what they find easy or difficult. They understand the demands of a particular learning task and are able to identify different approaches they could use to tackle a problem. Metacognitive learners are also able to make adjustments to their learning as they monitor their progress towards a particular learning goal.

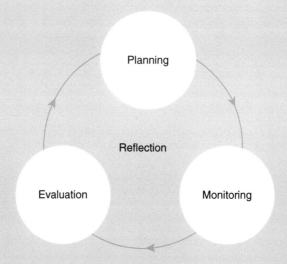

**Figure 8.1:** A helpful way to think about the phases involved in metacognition.

During the *planning* phase, students think about the explicit learning goal we have set and what we are asking them to do. As teachers, we need to make clear to students what success looks like in any given task before they embark on it. Students build on their prior knowledge, reflect on strategies they have used before and consider how they will approach the new task.

As students put their plan into action, they are constantly *monitoring* the progress they are making towards their learning goal. If the strategies they had decided to use are not working, they may decide to try something different.

Once they have completed the task, students determine how successful the strategy they used was in helping them to achieve their learning goal. During this *evaluation* phase, students think about what went well and what didn't go as well to help them decide what they could do differently next time. They may also think about what other types of problems they could solve using the same strategy.

*Reflection* is a fundamental part of the plan–monitor–evaluate process and there are various ways in which we can support our students to reflect on their learning process. In order to apply a metacognitive approach, students need access to a set of strategies that they can use and a classroom environment that encourages them to explore and develop their metacognitive skills.

# Why teach metacognitive skills?

Research evidence suggests that the use of metacognitive skills plays an important role in successful learning. Metacognitive practices help students to monitor their own progress and take control of their learning. Metacognitive learners think about and learn from their mistakes and modify their learning strategies accordingly. Students who use metacognitive techniques find it improves their academic achievement across subjects, as it helps them transfer what they have learnt from one context to another context, or from a previous task to a new task.

# What are the challenges of developing students' metacognitive skills?

For metacognition to be commonplace in the classroom, we need to encourage students to take time to think about and learn from their mistakes. Many students are afraid to make mistakes, meaning that they are less likely to take risks, explore new ways of thinking or tackle unfamiliar problems. We as teachers are instrumental in shaping the culture of learning in a classroom. For metacognitive practices to thrive, students need to feel confident enough to make mistakes, to discuss their mistakes and ultimately to view them as valuable, and often necessary, learning opportunities.

# Science is more than just facts

Some students may see Science as a fixed body of facts and rules that describe and explain how the world works, thinking that learning and applying them leads to success. However, Science is more than this: it is a way of thinking, of approaching problems, asking questions and finding the right way to answer them. A look at Science as a discipline can provide a starting point to promote all the metacognitive strategies we wish students to develop. This is a complex and contested area, but a simplified view of the nature of Science considers three connected domains (see Figure 8.2).

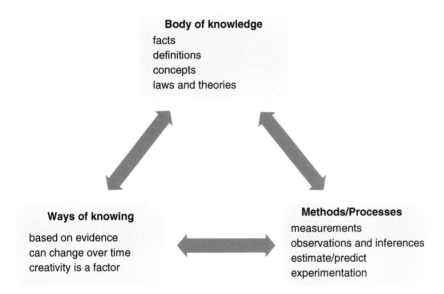

**Figure 8.2:** The nature of Science: knowledge, methods and ways of knowing.

The value in using this representation with students is that it helps them to develop a fuller understanding of what Science is and what it means to be good at it. The 'ways of knowing' domain can be rather abstract and less well defined in school Science so it is suggested that you initially focus on the other two, where it can be relatively easy for students to separate out the knowledge from the methods and processes when they are considering their own learning in Science.

> **☑ LESSON IDEA ONLINE 8.1: REVISION AND METACOGNITION**
>
> Use Lesson idea 8.1 to help students to consider the work they have done in a recent topic. What is the nature of that learning and in what different ways could the topic be learnt and assessed?

# Knowing that you have choices

It is easy for students to think that there is only one way to learn something or one 'right' answer to every question. If we want them to take responsibility for aspects of their learning, then they need to realise that there can be choices in what and how they learn, and we should plan to create opportunities for these choices inside and outside lessons.

> **LESSON IDEA 8.2: STUDENT CHOICES**
>
> For an upcoming lesson, plan multiple different activities to support learning (e.g. demonstration, practical, discussion, written task). The students choose which one they do and at the end of the lesson they talk with each other (and you) about their experiences and the relative strengths and limitations of each activity.

We can use model answers to help where possible, showing that a question can be answered correctly in different ways. Examples in Science of how understanding can be shown in different ways might include:

- A biological process such as digestion being represented by a free text description, a role play or annotated diagram(s).
- The motion of an object represented with graphs, using equations or as a cartoon strip showing positions of the objects every second.
- A chemical reaction represented by a symbol equation, a word equation or with three-dimensional molecular models.

Once students become familiar with these ideas, they will find it easier to ask themselves the kind of metacognitive questions we want, such as:

- **Planning (before).** Have I done something like this before? What do I need to know? Where should I start?
- **Monitoring (during).** How am I doing? What could I do differently? How can I get help?
- **Evaluation (after).** What worked well? How could I have done it better? What will I do differently next time?

---

Teacher Tip

Rather than asking for a single answer, set a problem and ask: *'How many different ways could you answer this question?'*

---

# Practical work, effective learning and self-evaluation

The planning phase of the self-regulation cycle (metacognition cycle) requires students to think about their learning goal and consider how they will approach the task. As teachers, we consider this every time we plan lessons, knowing why we pick activities, but how often do we share this thinking with the class?

## LESSON IDEA 8.3: ASSESSING CLASS EXPERIENCE

At the end of a lesson, ask all the students to write down what they thought the most important scientific ideas were, and for each idea, how confident they are that they understood it. This allows you to see if your intended learning goals are matched by the class experience.

We can use ideas from the research on practical work to help us and our classes to develop confidence in assessing how effective an activity is. Research from Millar *et al.* (1999) has proposed a model to help teachers consider the effectiveness of practical work, as shown in Figure 8.3.

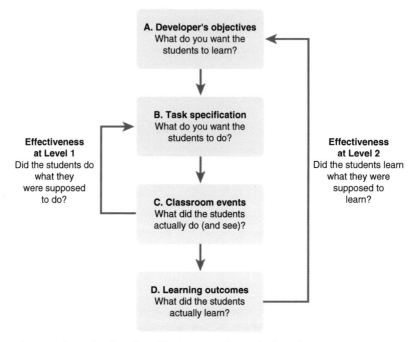

**Figure 8.3:** Evaluating the effectiveness of practical work.

---

Teacher Tip

The book *Enhancing Learning with Effective Practical Science 11–16* by Abrahams and Reiss (2017) has more detail on this framework (Chapters 1 and 2) and then 72 lesson guides which show how an applied version of this framework can be applied across common practical lessons in Biology, Chemistry and Physics (Chapters 3–8).

---

This framework can help teachers and students evaluate the effectiveness of a practical by separating out success in the doing (Level 1) from success in the learning (Level 2). It can help us ask questions about our teaching and it can help students pose questions about their learning. Some of these questions might look like this:

- What was the point of this practical?
- Did things go to plan and did I get the results I expected?
- If not, what went wrong? Something I did, the equipment or something else?

- What are the key Science ideas in this practical?
- How well did this practical help me learn them?
- Are there any other ways I could learn these ideas?

---

**Teacher Tip**

Ask students some or all of the questions above after a practical activity. You can compare their responses to what you think they should be.

---

Asking students to critique a lesson may make them feel uncomfortable and we might take criticism personally. However, if we set the right atmosphere, this can be valuable, and by providing opportunities to get students to evaluate their own learning against what we had planned, we can help them to be more autonomous, self-regulated learners.

Feedback is very important, but we usually see this as something from the teacher to student. In the book *Visible Learning* (2009), John Hattie makes a critical point about the direction of feedback:

'It was only when I discovered that feedback was most powerful when it is **from the student to the teacher** that I started to understand it better. When teachers seek, or are at least open to, feedback from students as to what students know, what they understand, where they make errors, when they have misconceptions – then teaching and learning can be synchronised and powerful.'

Asking for feedback from students helps them develop as metacognitive learners and make decisions about what they might do differently next time. This can form part of the evaluation section of the self-regulation cycle. It also helps us to reflect on and improve our own teaching, benefiting everyone.

# Learning in small steps

We want students to ask questions like, 'Is this strategy working for me?' or 'Might I need to try to answer this question in a different way?' However, they can only do so if they know how well they are doing. Chapter 7 **Assessment for Learning** suggests ways to assess understanding, but learning is more of an incremental process than something that happens in big steps. As a result, we need to consider these steps on the way to fully understanding something, and build this into our teaching.

Many ideas in Science are hierarchical and require some prior understanding to allow us to move on. Understanding the difference between meiosis and mitosis requires knowing about cells and their nature. In electricity, to understand Ohm's law you need to be confident with the ideas of potential difference, current and resistance.

---

**LESSON IDEA ONLINE 8.4: PROGRESSION OF IDEAS, SELF-CONFIDENCE AND REVISION CHECKLISTS**

As part of a revision lesson, give students the main topic (e.g. chemical bonding, human systems, electrical circuits) and ask them to write down the key ideas and arrange them in order of progression or difficulty. Pre-prepared cards may help some groups with this task. See Lesson idea 8.4 for more details.

---

When planning lessons, we should consider these steps to a full understanding and build in interim questions and activities. This will help students to see what they know so that they are able to consider the next steps.

---

**Teacher Tip**

Print out the syllabus content for one of the topics you are teaching and cut it into pieces, one for each concept. Shuffle these and rearrange in the way that you think makes the most sense for teaching. Compare this to the scheme of work or ask a colleague to do the same thing and see if you want to revise the sequencing of lessons into a more logical, hierarchical structure.

---

# There is more than one way to take notes

To develop metacognitive strategies, we need to move some responsibility to the students, empowering them to make decisions about their own learning. Making these choices can feel daunting for students so a good starting point is something that they are familiar with: taking notes.

Students may not have been taught how to take notes or realise that there are different ways that may work better in different situations. One example is the Cornell note-taking method (see Figure 8.4), designed to make students identify the key ideas and review their own work.

| Cue column | Notes column |
|---|---|
| You write key words and questions here | You write notes here |
| Summary | |
| You write a summary here at the end | |

**Figure 8.4:** The Cornell note-taking method.

You might want to ask the whole class to try this technique first and get them to talk about what they like and what they don't, before letting them pick their own note-taking method.

## LESSON IDEA 8.5: CREATIVE RECORDING

Tell the class that for a few lessons you will not give them notes and that they must decide the best way to record the important ideas. Encourage students to be as creative as possible. Allow them time in the lesson to write the notes, perhaps in groups. Afterwards, they share their experiences about what worked best for them and what they might do in the future.

# Revise all year, not just before the test

Many students revise for tests at the last minute, even though this may not be effective. Research from cognitive psychology suggests an effective way to remember things is with regular practice testing throughout the year. These tests can be short and the students can write the questions themselves.

---

### Teacher Tip

The article 'Strengthening the Student Toolbox' by John Dunlosky (2013) is freely available and describes how effective different study strategies are. Read it, discuss it with colleagues and share some of the ideas with your students.

---

After each lesson, students could make flash cards with key ideas on one side and question(s) on the other, using these to test themselves regularly. The Leitner system is one way to organise these cards and help students test themselves most often on the things that they find hardest to remember.

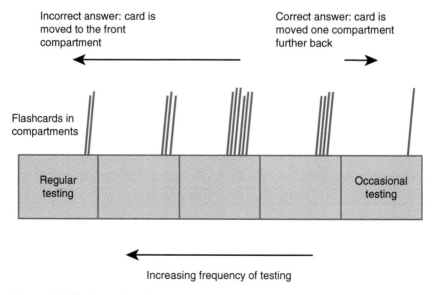

**Figure 8.5:** Flash card testing.

This approach allows students to monitor their own progress. If all the cards are moving to the back, their revision plans are working; if not, they may want to change the plans. However, it is only one way to help students learn and revise and it may be that different parts of the Science course are better suited to different methods. This may work well for learning equations in Physics, but annotated diagrams might work better for biological systems and worked examples could be better for balancing equations in Chemistry. In the evaluation phase of the self-regulation cycle, the choice should belong to the student.

# Questions and metacognition

Metacognition is not just 'thinking about thinking', it is about understanding and actively monitoring one's learning and changing behaviours if needed. One way to model the kind of good Science thinking we want is 'thinking aloud'. In class, before you do something to help students learn, explain why, perhaps with questions. For example, if you were looking at the forces on an object, rather than immediately drawing a diagram, say to the class something like 'This is a complex situation with different forces in different directions; what's the best way to help me answer this question and why?'

Good questions that we'd like the students to ask themselves include:

- What are the scientific ideas needed for this question?
- Are there any equations/laws I need?
- Can I remember these or do I need to look them up?
- When I am finished, how will I know if I am right?

The answers may seem obvious to us, but that is because we are already the expert that we want the students to become. By modelling best practice, we show students what we'd like them to be able to do themselves.

**Teacher Tip**

After an activity in a lesson, ask the class to say why they think you taught it that way. You can compare their reasons to yours, and perhaps even see if they have better ideas for next time!

**Summary**

There are two dimensions to metacognition that we want to encourage and this chapter has provided examples to support you and your students in considering both:

- **Metacognitive knowledge** is what students know about effective learning as well as what works best for them in different situations, for example, note taking and revision strategies.

- **Metacognitive regulation** is the process by which students plan, monitor and evaluate their own learning, assessing how they are doing and changing what they do if needed, for example, evaluating the effectiveness of practical work.

# Language awareness

9

# What is language awareness?

For many students, English is an additional language. It might be their second or perhaps their third language. Depending on the school context, students might be learning all or just some of their subjects through English.

For all students, regardless of whether they are learning through their first language or an additional language, language is a vehicle for learning. It is through language that students access the learning intentions of the lesson and communicate their ideas. It is our responsibility as teachers to ensure that language doesn't present a barrier to learning.

One way to achieve this is to support our colleagues in becoming more language-aware. Language awareness is sensitivity to, and an understanding of, the language demands of our subject and the role these demands play in learning. A language-aware teacher plans strategies and scaffolds the appropriate support to help students overcome these language demands.

# Why is it important for teachers of other subjects to be language-aware?

Many teachers are surprised when they receive a piece of written work that suggests a student who has no difficulties in everyday communication has had problems understanding the lesson. Issues arise when teachers assume that students who have attained a high degree of fluency and accuracy in everyday social English therefore have a corresponding level of academic language proficiency. Whether English is a student's first language or an additional language, students need time and the appropriate support to become proficient in academic language. This is the language that they are mostly exposed to in school and will be required to reproduce themselves. It will also scaffold their ability to access higher order thinking skills and improve levels of attainment.

# What are the challenges of language awareness?

Many teachers of non-language subjects worry that there is no time to factor language support into their lessons, or that language is something they know little about. Some teachers may think that language support is not their role. However, we need to work with these teachers to create inclusive classrooms where all students can access the curriculum and where barriers to learning are reduced as much as possible. An increased awareness of the language needs of students aims to reduce any obstacles that learning through an additional language might present.

This doesn't mean that all teachers need to know the names of grammatical structures or need to be able to use the appropriate linguistic labels. What it does mean is that we all need to understand the challenges our students face, including their language level, and plan some strategies to help them overcome these challenges. These strategies do not need to take a lot of additional time and should eventually become integral to our process of planning, teaching and reflecting on our practice. We may need to support other teachers so that they are clear about the vocabulary and language that is specific to their subject, and how to teach, reinforce and develop it.

# Language and Science learning

Language is central to Science and Science teaching. When scientists think about natural phenomena, they use language to refer to key concepts like velocity, and abstract ideas like electric current. They use analogies to make sense of abstract ideas, comparing electric current to the flow of water. When testing ideas, they use language to frame hypotheses and to communicate their findings. In doing so, they use a specialised vocabulary, alternative communication devices like graphs, mathematics, tables, symbols and diagrams, and conventions of writing and vocabulary very specific to Science. Without language, scientific ideas cannot be constructed.

If you teach Science in English to students with English as an additional language (EAL), you are doing something called content and language integrated learning (CLIL). As the name suggests, whether you like it or not, you are helping students to learn Science and English at the same time. Because the language of Science can seem foreign and complex, learning Science can itself be like learning a language. You may never have thought about it, but you are teaching Science to students who are learning the language of Science at the same time.

# Difficulties with the language of Science

Language is our main tool for helping students to learn Science, but that doesn't mean it's easy! The language of Science can be very challenging for students, and Science can seem very difficult to understand as a result. There are various reasons for this:

1   There is complex scientific terminology (like electron, particle and photosynthesis); in addition, because of the way scientists build scientific theories, there are lots of words that mean something different in Science than in everyday life (like respiration, weight and force). In fact, research suggests that at least six new words are introduced into each GCSE Science lesson. Everyday English words

that are used in the context of Science can cause as much difficulty for students as scientific words. Words like abundant, random, contrast, linear and incident can be particularly problematic. Trying to understand the meaning of familiar words in a different context is a challenge for students, particularly for those with EAL.

---

### Teacher Tip

Choose your words carefully. For example, don't say electricity when you mean electric current. The context of the sentence may make it clear, but if your students are struggling to understand the whole sentence, you need to be unambiguous.

---

2   Logical connectives are the next problem. These are words that suggest addition ('Add the Benedict's solution **and** put the tube in the water bath'), opposition ('Do the experiment in a fume hood, **otherwise** smoke will escape into the room'), cause ('We add the Universal indicator **because** we want to measure the pH') and time ('Add the hydrochloric acid. **After** that, add the magnesium'). They are essential to constructing a scientific argument, because they help establish relationships between claims and data, and they are used to compare and contrast phenomena. But students find text with logical connectives hard to understand.

---

### Teacher Tip

You can't avoid the use of logical connectives because of their fundamental purpose in justifying scientific claims. Instead, spend time helping students to identify the connectives and understand the meaning they convey.

---

3   The language of Science does not just involve words. Students also build their understanding through graphs, Maths, equations, symbols and diagrams. This multimodal form can be helpful to students' understanding. Imagine how hard it would be to use just words to teach the structure of the lungs, whereas a diagram makes things easier. However, when Mathematics is needed to make the ideas clear, particularly in Physics, this may create new barriers.

---

**Teacher Tip**

If you ask students to draw a graph, or use Mathematics, you will know it can take a long time. Even though they can do it quickly in a Maths lesson, the ability to transfer Maths skills to Science is a problem recognised in educational research, and you must include time during the lesson to support students.

---

4   Scientific reports are often written in the passive voice (for example, '5g of copper sulphate was taken'). This is deliberate, as it conveys the idea of objective truth. But students can find it difficult, inaccessible and discouraging.

---

**Teacher Tip**

Allow your students to write up practical reports in the first person (sentences are likely to start with 'I' or 'We').

---

# Supporting students' use of language in Science

So how can you support your students in using language in Science classrooms, and in adopting the language of Science? Let's focus on talk, reading and writing.

## Talk

Robin Alexander, Professor of Education at the University of Cambridge, said: 'Children, we now know, need to experience a rich diet of spoken language in order to think and to learn.' However, if you're like many other teachers, it's likely that most of the talk in your lessons is your own.

Usually we ask questions that we already know the answer to, students answer, and we tell them if they're right or wrong. But often that means they are only using basic conversational language, without using and developing their knowledge of scientific language in their answers. So how can you make talk active, and involve students in real discussion, using appropriate scientific language?

- Use open-ended questions starting with 'How?' and 'Why?' to help extend students' thinking using talk. For example, *'Why do you think the rate of reaction increases with temperature?'*
- Comment on students' responses to check meaning, but ask other students to comment on the content of their answers, or build upon these answers.
- Use group work, but give students clear roles, expectations and responsibilities, so that everyone has an obligation to contribute to the group's discussions. Give the work a purpose, such as solving a problem or building knowledge towards some other aim.
- Use a concept cartoon to encourage classroom dialogue. You may use cartoon in Figure 9.1. Ask students to say who they agree with, and to justify their answer. Involve several students with contrasting views, and build the discussion towards consensus.

**Figure 9.1:** A concept cartoon.

- Build in peer–peer discussions, or ask peers to teach, or present to, their peers.

- Give students thinking time after asking a question to ensure answers are of sufficient quality; do not rush to prompt a poorly thought-out answer.
- Encourage participation from everyone by choosing students to contribute to class discussion with a random name generator, rather than just accepting answers from those with their hands up.
- Give praise in response to students' talk, using their contributions to build the discussion, and enhancing their self-confidence in talking.

---

**☑ LESSON IDEA ONLINE 9.1: CONCEPT CARTOONS**

Use a concept cartoon to help explore a common student misconception. Ask which students agree with each of the opinions in the cartoon. Ask like-minded students to pair up, and to think together about why they agree with their chosen opinion, and how they would persuade someone of their view.

---

Many of us worry about students talking in pairs or groups because we're afraid students will go off-task, or that the dynamics of the group simply won't work. There's nothing wrong with feeling like this, but it helps to make sure that expectations and time limits are clear, and to ask students to make a list of rules for group discussion. An example list is as follows:

- Give everyone a chance to speak.
- Listen to people without interrupting.
- Be prepared to change your mind.
- Come to a consensus after talking.
- Explain ideas clearly, giving reasons for what you say.
- Actively listen and be open to new ideas.

It is also helpful to improve your use of particular talk and grouping strategies:

- **Pair talk.** This is ideal to promote high levels of participation and to ensure that the discussions are highly focused, especially if there are tight deadlines. Use it to help students recall work from a previous lesson, generate questions or plan a piece of writing. It is ideal for quick-fire reflection and review, and for going through ideas before presenting them to the whole class.

- **Two to four.** Get students to work together in pairs, then join the pairs up into fours to explain and compare ideas.
- **Listening triads.** Get students to work in groups of three. Each student takes on the role of talker, questioner or recorder. The talker explains something. The questioner prompts and seeks clarification. The recorder takes notes and reports back on the conversation later.
- **Envoys.** Once groups have carried out a task, get one person from each group (the envoy) to move to a new group to explain and summarise, and to find out what the new group thought, or how they carried out the task. This envoy should then return to the original group and feed back. This is an effective way of avoiding tedious and repetitive 'reporting back' sessions. It also forces the envoys to think about their use of language and helps develop active listening.
- **Snowball.** Pairs discuss an issue or idea, then double up to fours and continue the process, then double up to eights in order to compare ideas, choose the best ideas or come to a consensus. Finally, the whole class is drawn together and spokespeople for each group of eight feed back the outcomes of the discussions.
- **Rainbow.** After small groups have discussed together, give students a number, shape or colour (try hiding it under their chairs before the lesson!). Students with the same number or colour join up, making groups with representatives of each original group. In their new group, students take turns to report back on their group's work, forming a new, combined task.
- **Jigsaw.** A topic is divided into sections. In groups of four or five, students take a section each, and then regroup into 'expert' groups. In these groups, experts work together on their chosen area. Students then return to their original groups to report back. The original group is then given a task that requires the students to use the different areas of 'expertise' for a joint outcome.
- **Spokesperson.** Each group appoints a spokesperson. Ask each group in turn to offer one new point to the discussion. Alternatively, you can ask groups to summarise their findings on A3 sheets, which are then displayed. The class then compares and comments on them.

Whatever strategies you use, remember that talk provides students with a means of thinking together to jointly build up their understanding of ideas.

# Reading

Think about your classroom. How long do your students spend reading? A recent study found that reading occupied less than 10% of lesson time in Science. Students should be able to build ideas from reading scientific writing. To do so, they need to develop skills in reflective reading, where they may read, re-read and reflect upon text to build connections with prior knowledge and reinforce their learning. Reading activities which can help to build learning, and build students' skills in reflective reading, are called Directed Activities Related to Text (DARTs).

In DARTS, students deconstruct or construct text to help them understand it. DARTS provide a useful scaffold for students learning through an additional language. Try some of the following in your teaching!

- **Completing text, tables or diagrams.** Get students to: complete deleted words or phrases in sentences; complete missing labels on diagrams, using a piece of text for information; complete a table, using a piece of text for information.
- **Sequencing and classifying pieces of text into categories.** Ask students to: rearrange a set of instructions, or a sequence of events in a biological process, to put them in the correct order; classify pieces of text into categories.
- **Matching.** Ask students to match key words to definitions or to components on a diagram.
- **Predicting.** Give students sentences with missing words at the end. Students predict the missing words and complete the sentences.
- **Labelling and highlighting.** Ask students to: highlight key words in a piece of text (e.g. the endocrine glands in a passage about homeostasis); label parts of the text with labels provided (e.g. label the forces mentioned in a piece of text); or break the text down into segments and then label the segments (e.g. break the text down into logical steps).
- **Recording and constructing.** Ask students to: build a table, using information given in a piece of text; answer questions about a piece of text set by a teacher; make up a set of questions about a piece of text; condense a piece of text into a set of key points; reconstruct a piece of text to show the interrelationship between ideas by producing a flow chart, branching diagram, a concept map or other graphic organiser.

**LESSON IDEA 9.2: ENGAGING WITH MARK SCHEMES**
Give students the mark scheme for an examination paper. In groups of three, ask them to read the mark scheme and think about what the original examination questions were. By reading each point, they engage with the learning intended, reflecting on what they read to draw conclusions.

# Writing

We all know that parents like to see writing in exercise books or on paper. If their children are writing things down, they are working hard! However, it's important to think about the purpose of writing in your lessons. Do you ask students to copy from the board, or to listen to your dictation? This won't get them to think about the ideas. But they **will** learn if they have to think while doing the writing – then writing becomes a learning activity.

In fact, writing can be classified into three main types, with some writing activities falling into more than one type:

1  **Writing to learn.** Being asked to write forces students to choose words, and then to link them together in a meaningful way. The process of writing helps them to formulate their ideas and gradually build ideas upon other ideas. Here are some examples:

   - answering questions about a piece of text or a diagram
   - justifying a decision, such as classifying an animal into a particular group
   - breaking down big ideas
   - relating function and process
   - ordering and classifying pieces of students' writing
   - preparing a summary
   - converting a diagram into words and vice versa
   - taking notes from a textbook (if students are thinking as they write!)
   - writing questions for an end-of-lesson quiz
   - constructing a graphic organiser from a piece of text.

These kinds of activities do not just allow students to build scientific concepts. They also allow students to work within a second or third language, with the activities themselves helping students to use, clarify and refine their English.

**☑ LESSON IDEA ONLINE 9.3: WRITING A SOUNDTRACK**

Asking students to write a soundtrack to a video is an engaging approach when introducing a topic. This approach can also be used when assessing students' understanding or asking them to apply prior learning.

2 **Writing to reason.** Using writing to analyse and criticise evidence, and to synthesise and evaluate ideas, can enable students to engage in reasoning, where they construct an argument using the data to help make conclusions. You can help them to do that by providing writing frames to help structure their thinking and use of language (see Table 9.1).

| Aim |
|---|
| What is the aim? |
| Why are we studying it? |
| **Hypothesis** |
| What is the hypothesis? |
| **Method** |
| What data did you collect? |
| How did you collect it? |
| How did you stay safe? |
| **Results** |
| Present your results in a table. |
| Choose and draw an appropriate graph. |
| **Conclusions** |
| What does your data show? |
| Was your hypothesis supported? How do you know? |

**Table 9.1:** A writing frame to help structure reasoning.

3 **Writing to communicate.** When students write, they often write in order to get the marks. But this can constrain their writing

approach, and it is worth changing the audience and changing the writing tasks to get them to write more genuinely. Try some of the following writing tasks in your classroom:

- poetry
- storytelling (e.g. about the journey of a cellulose molecule from mouth to anus)
- concept maps (to outline and clarify their understanding)
- storyboards (e.g. to help sequence a scientific process)
- cartoons (e.g. to represent an abstract concept)
- posters (by working together on a shared writing aim, students can support each other)
- blogs, collaborative documents or web pages
- letters
- biography
- playscript
- newspaper articles
- diary entries.

By allowing students to write expressively or poetically, you increase the chances that the writing will convey their understanding, particularly when they apply their learning to a different form of writing.

Of course, all three forms of writing can help to expose students' ideas, both to themselves and to you, helping you to assess and make decisions about what to teach next. If students find it difficult to write, this may suggest their ideas are wrong and force them to re-think the ideas, and how the ideas fit together. It may also suggest that they require additional support with English language learning. Giving your students writing tasks can really help them to learn.

## Teacher Tip

Next time you ask students to talk, read or write, ask yourself why you are doing it. Are you asking them to communicate before they understand a topic? Does your writing demand thinking? Does the talking in your class allow students to think together? Sometimes students do not like writing, so make sure that when they do it, you have a good rationale for it.

# Lowering the scientific language barrier for EAL students

When you teach Science to students with English as an additional language, you can't help being a teacher of English too. Much of the language awareness already discussed will serve you well with this group of students, but in this section you can find some additional strategies which may be useful.

## Initiation

Build up a bilingual dictionary of scientific words and pictures (Figure 9.2), and encourage students to carry around a normal dictionary or use an online translation service whenever needed. Allocate a 'buddy' to a student with limited English, for support. Don't expect a student with EAL to speak a lot for some time – it can be intimidating. Even though they don't speak, they may still be learning a lot. Equally, don't be surprised if you receive a piece of written work from a student who has no difficulties in everyday communication but who has struggled to demonstrate their learning in a written task. Problems arise when teachers assume that students who have attained a high degree of fluency and accuracy in everyday social English have a corresponding level of academic proficiency. Also, students can have differing levels of proficiency (and confidence) across the four skills (reading; writing; speaking; listening) – in a first and additional language.

---

**LESSON IDEA 9.4: BILINGUAL DICTIONARIES**

Use a bilingual dictionary of scientific laboratory equipment to help all students understand what each piece of equipment looks like.

---

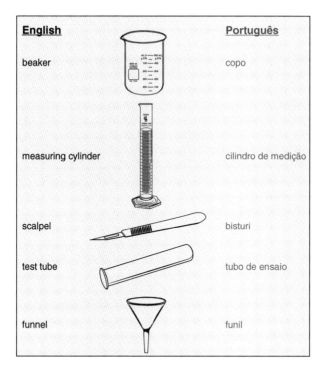

| English | | Português |
|---|---|---|
| beaker | | copo |
| measuring cylinder | | cilindro de medição |
| scalpel | | bisturi |
| test tube | | tubo de ensaio |
| funnel | | funil |

**Figure 9.2:** A bilingual dictionary of scientific laboratory equipment.

# Orientation

Start with what students already know. Recap prior learning or refer to other contexts which exemplify the scientific language and content. Relate ideas to previous lessons and lesson experiences. Help students to make connections with previous learning. Be explicit about the language needed to learn about the topic. This may include specialist terminology, or even words that change their meaning between subjects (such as force or respiration).

# Speaking

If you are talking about something, show an example. Demonstrate a process or idea while you are talking about it. Position yourself where you can be heard and where you can see everybody's faces to check they understand. Use precise terms, rather than vague ones, so students can understand easily. Maintain eye contact – students can understand meaning from your facial expressions. Keep your volume down so you don't shout. Ensure students have breaks from listening to you. Repeat important points and put them on the board. Ask students to summarise what you've said. Avoid metaphors, which students may not understand, unless you explain them. Avoid slang or jargon, and take time to think about the language you use to make it precise. Phrase questions in alternative ways to help comprehension.

## Writing

Some students may still be getting used to writing in a different script. Encourage students to write collaboratively in order to learn from each other. Use Google docs or another cloud computing application so they can edit a document simultaneously. Provide students with writing frames to help them structure their writing, whatever its purpose.

## Reading

When reading, some students may still be growing accustomed to the sounds made by letters in English. They may not be able to recognise the key words which carry the most information in a piece of text. They may not recognise when one word has been substituted for another, such as the emboldened words in these examples: 'Measure 10 ml of 1M hydrochloric acid. Add **it** to the beaker.'; 'Find the bar magnets; take **one** and attach it to the side of the vehicle.' They may find it difficult to understand sentences with connectives. Focus on the connectives, and try to use precise language in the text you give to students.

### Summary

- Language is an important tool in helping students to learn Science.

- You must focus on talking, reading and writing to help students think and learn.

- Help your learners with English as an additional language by making adjustments to your practice in initiation, orientation, talking, reading and writing.

# Inclusive education

10

# What is inclusive education?

Individual differences among students will always exist; our challenge as teachers is to see these not as problems to be fixed but as opportunities to enrich and make learning accessible for all. Inclusion is an effort to make sure all students receive whatever specially designed instruction and support they need to succeed as learners.

An inclusive teacher welcomes all students and finds ways to accept and accommodate each individual student. An inclusive teacher identifies existing barriers that limit access to learning, then finds solutions and strategies to remove or reduce those barriers. Some barriers to inclusion are visible; others are hidden or difficult to recognise.

Barriers to inclusion might be the lack of educational resources available for teachers or an inflexible curriculum that does not take into account the learning differences that exist among all learners, across all ages. We also need to encourage students to understand each others' barriers, or this itself may become a barrier to learning.

Students may experience challenges because of any one or a combination of the following:

- behavioural and social skill difficulties
- communication or language disabilities
- concentration difficulties
- conflict in the home or that caused by political situations or national emergency
- executive functions, such as difficulties in understanding, planning and organising
- hearing impairments, acquired congenitally or through illness or injury
- literacy and language difficulties
- numeracy difficulties
- physical or neurological impairments, which may or may not be visible
- visual impairments, ranging from mild to severe.

We should be careful, however, not to label a student and create further barriers in so doing, particularly if we ourselves are not qualified to make a diagnosis. Each child is unique but it is our management of their learning environment that will decide the extent of the barrier and the need for it to be a factor. We need to be aware of a child's readiness to learn and their readiness for school.

# Why is inclusive education important?

Teachers need to find ways to welcome all students and organise their teaching so that each student gets a learning experience that makes engagement and success possible. We should create a good match between what we teach and how we teach it, and what the student needs and is capable of. We need not only to ensure access but also make sure each student receives the support and individual attention that result in meaningful learning.

# What are the challenges of an inclusive classroom?

Some students may have unexpected barriers. Those who consistently do well in class may not perform in exams, or those who are strong at writing may be weaker when speaking. Those who are considered to be the brightest students may also have barriers to learning. Some students may be working extra hard to compensate for barriers they prefer to keep hidden; some students may suddenly reveal limitations in their ability to learn, using the techniques they have been taught. We need to be aware of all corners of our classroom, be open and put ourselves in our students' shoes.

# Creating an inclusive Science classroom

Establishing an inclusive approach to teaching and learning in Science should underpin your practice and support all students' learning, whether they have a recognised barrier to learning or not. In fact, creating an inclusive classroom is simply creating a space where good Science teaching and learning can happen.

## Begin at the students' starting points

Take time to work out the starting points of your students and build from there. You could use a starter activity to assess prior learning, or a plenary activity in the previous lesson to help you plan the next lesson. Set learning activities in everyday contexts, such as cars, the human body, local ecosystems, etc. A familiar setting can provide students with a recognisable starting point to build their knowledge on.

## Make your students do the learning

Give your students activities they will learn from, rather than trying to teach them as if one size fits all (you have already met lots of ideas earlier in this book). They should spend most of the time working independently, rather than just listening to you. Ensure your activities have broken down the process of learning into step-by-step procedures which are manageable by all of your students. Think about the different levels of knowledge students must work through.

## Activate peers as educational resources for each other

Students can often explain complex scientific ideas to each other more effectively than you can. They understand each other's difficulties and they speak in the same language as their peers. Create learning activities that encourage peer support, rather than insisting on silence – not least because it will make the lesson easier for you to manage!

# Give yourself a chance to help those that need it

When you run a discussion as a class, you cannot cater for every student's difficulties. You definitely cannot do it if you only lecture your class from the front. By giving students activities to do, you make yourself available to provide support to those who need it. This includes those with barriers to learning, and those who find things very easy and need additional stretch and challenge. When you do provide support, you may be simply asking the right question to help a student progress, or you may be adjusting the task or outcome to make it more achievable. Sometimes, you may decide not to intervene, to allow a student to puzzle something out by themselves.

# Allow everyone to experience success

If you are writing a worksheet, start with the easier questions to give students a sense that they can do it. Praise students' achievements and answers to questions, however insignificant, in a targeted way. Don't just say 'well done' constantly as it will become devalued. You could say, *'Excellent graph – well-chosen scales on the axes!'* You could use your tone of voice to show how you value their work, or you could even use their answer to develop the next stage in a discussion. This type of feedback gives students the sense that their efforts are valued, and will help them to develop a belief in their own abilities.

# Don't be afraid to change your plans

If the lesson is not working out and no-one understands, don't ignore it and continue. Stop the lesson if necessary and ask questions to find out what students' problems are, resolve the problems and then set the students working again. You may need to modify or explain the words you have used, provide more time, move students into different groups or direct students to different resources. Monitoring students' understanding throughout the lesson is essential. It enables you to target your support and adjust your plans in order to respond to your students' needs.

---

**Teacher Tip**

Keep just one of these considerations in your mind as you plan and teach each lesson. Building an inclusive classroom is not easy, and reflecting on your success in a targeted way can be very helpful.

---

# Thinking about differentiation

Even if you adopt these inclusive approaches, supporting all students' learning at the same time is difficult. All students can be engaged in meaningful activities that can promote learning. But not all students will be engaged by and learn from every activity. And students may learn differently, and different things, from the same activity. Once you've worked out what students need to learn, you may decide to adopt one of the following approaches to differentiate learning activities for different students:

1  **Differentiation by task.** Here you design different tasks for different students. You may, for example, produce core tasks (for everyone) and harder tasks (for the higher achievers). These tasks can lead students to the same, or different, learning outcomes. You may allocate tasks to different students or allow them to choose. In designing different activities, you may need to:

   • adjust the scientific skills and mathematical skills required
   • adjust the level of oral and written skills required
   • present instructions in different ways, such as written, diagrammatic, oral or video
   • vary the degree of independence given to students
   • produce graded tasks, which start easy and get more difficult
   • vary the questions which are asked, perhaps drawing on Bloom's Taxonomy (see Table 10.1) to help increase or lower the level of demand

- adjust how you ask students to record their learning; rather than always being required to write, students could give oral or video presentations, create animations and so on.

---

**☑ LESSON IDEA ONLINE 10.1: DIFFERENTIATING BY TASK**

You can differentiate by task by using different learning objectives with different students, or by changing the level of difficulty of the task, with different tasks for different students.

---

2 **Differentiation by outcome.** Here, you give everyone the same task, but it's designed to allow students to achieve the outcome in different ways depending on their individual level. For example, you may ask students to create an information leaflet about the breathing system. Students will approach this in lots of different ways, with some including more information, and engaging with it at a higher level than others. This can be a more inclusive approach, as it avoids unintentionally 'labelling' students when you give them different tasks.

---

**☑ LESSON IDEA ONLINE 10.2: DIFFERENTIATING BY OUTCOME**

Students do the same task, but they may complete it to different levels. It also provides opportunity for differentiation by working in groups, so students can support each other, and so you can circulate around the class, asking questions to develop students' ideas.

---

3 **Differentiation by route.** Here, you ask students to work in groups to produce a shared outcome, but different students take different roles (according to their strengths) in producing the outcome. For example, the task may be to produce a news report about climate change. Two students may take responsibility for researching and writing the script, one student for creating the storyboard and another for filming and editing, to make sure the story is clear.

| Know | describe, define, draw, identify, infer, label, list, locate, match, name, outline, recall, select, state, write |
|---|---|
| Comprehend | classify, confirm, compare, convert, demonstrate, estimate, explain, differentiate between, give examples, illustrate, interpret, translate |
| Apply | apply, change, compute, construct, demonstrate, determine, develop, model, modify, produce, solve, show, relate, use |
| Analyse | analyse, categorise, classify, compare, contrast, debate, diagram, differentiate, examine, illustrate, investigate, sort |
| Synthesise | build, combine, compile, construct, create, design, develop, discuss, formulate, imagine, invent, modify, predict, propose, solve |
| Evaluate | appraise, assess, choose, conclude, critique, deduct, estimate, justify, judge, prioritise |

**Table 10.1:** Bloom's Taxonomy and questions for learning.

Teacher Tip

Always think about what questions to ask when you plan the lesson, rather than asking unplanned questions off the top of your head during the lesson. Forward planning helps secure better learning.

# Overcoming barriers to learning

The sections which follow outline some of the strategies to help overcome barriers to learning in the Science classroom or laboratory. They include strategies for students who have special needs in communication and interaction; behaviour, emotional and social development; cognition and learning; alongside sensory, physical and medical needs. The advice in Tables 10.2–10.5 is adapted from work originally completed by the Association for Science Education and the National Association for Special Educational Needs.

---

**Teacher Tip**

Although it is useful to think of students' needs under categories, don't let the 'labels' mislead you. Expect a lot from all the students in your class, and provide them with support to help them meet your expectations.

---

# Communication and interaction

This category of needs may include students with dyslexia, dyspraxia, hearing impairment, autism, along with other severe or profound learning difficulties which affect communication. Many of the strategies in Table 10.2 will also be useful in supporting students' learning through an additional language (see Chapter 9 **Language awareness**).

| Help students to acquire and use scientific language | • Use word banks, with explanations of key words. |
|---|---|
| | • Practise saying scientific words as a class, and provide opportunities to discuss the meaning of words in pairs or small groups. |
| | • Visually link a word to its explanation, for example using flash cards, or link a name to a piece of apparatus. Use permanent displays which include matching pictures or labelled diagrams. |
| | • Break words down into their meanings, such as photo (light) synthesis (making). |
| | • Label shelves with the names of equipment stored there. |
| | • Think about the words you intend to use in a lesson, and ensure new words are noted by students and explained. |

→

| | |
|---|---|
| **Communicate with students in ways which replace or supplement language** | • Use physical movements and demonstrations to reinforce what you are saying. You might push and pull something to demonstrate forces, or use a sieve to help students understand absorption in the gut.<br><br>• Use images, graphs, pictures, diagrams, animations and photographs to make abstract ideas clear. For example, an animation of electrons orbiting the nucleus of an atom makes the structure much easier to understand.<br><br>• Give instructions in video or diagrammatic form, as well as orally and in written form. |
| **Think about the best ways to communicate scientific ideas** | • Plan your lessons so the steps in learning are clear. Don't introduce too many concepts at once.<br><br>• Give students the chance to communicate their learning in different ways, such as mind maps, animations or videos.<br><br>• Provide structured exercises, but also encourage more open writing to help students think more widely, for example 'You are a glucose molecule. Tell the story of your journey from a dinner plate to a cell.' |
| **Encourage a feeling of security** | • Once you find approaches that work, stick with them.<br><br>• People with autism do not like too much change and experimentation, and you may want to have a 'safe area' for them to retreat to when necessary. |

**Table 10.2:** Communication and interaction strategies.

# Behaviour, emotional and social development

This category of needs may include those who are withdrawn or isolated, disruptive or disturbing, hyperactive, lacking concentration or with immature social skills. Your challenge will be to balance the principle of ensuring students' involvement while minimising risk in the Science lab.

| Focus on safety | • Routines can be helpful: for example, having goggles in the same place and always getting goggles at the same point in a lesson. |
|---|---|
| | • Undertake a risk assessment to decide if a practical activity is suitable for groups with very challenging behaviour. For example, it may be unwise to use scalpels with some students. |
| | • Know the location of your 'STOP' button and shut-off valves in your laboratory. |
| Encourage positive behaviour and participation | • Celebrate good work. Give praise and display work on the classroom walls. |
| | • Allow students to report upon investigations and practical work in ways that don't involve writing, such as PowerPoint presentations, videos and so on. |
| | • Incorporate students' interests into lessons. For example, teaching forces through the context of skateboards may be more engaging than simply teaching forces. |
| | • Take photographs (if allowed by school policy) of students participating well, and display them on the classroom walls to value the behaviour. |
| | • Where a student has a keen interest or skill in something scientific, encourage their participation in lessons. For example, a lesson on sound could involve a student playing a musical instrument. |
| Reduce opportunities for poor behaviour or lack of concentration | • Think about where to put equipment to minimise students' opportunity to disrupt others while walking around the class, and to maintain their focus on their own work. |
| | • Start a practical activity at different times for different sets of students, to avoid crowds of students around equipment. |
| | • Choose which students should work together in groups, rather than letting groups form naturally, to prevent poor behaviour and encourage concentration. |

→

| Avoid students getting frustrated | • Step in quickly at the first sign of frustration.<br><br>• In an investigation, avoid saying that a prediction is wrong, as students may not realise this is a natural part of the investigation process.<br><br>• Plan, in advance, what action you will take if emotional outbursts happen. |
|---|---|
| Give the lesson structure | • Plan your lessons with distinctive sections, incorporating different types of activity, such as practical work, discussion and so on.<br><br>• Use learning activities where the instructions and outcomes are clear. Do not use open-ended investigations. |

**Table 10.3:** Ensuring students' involvement while minimising risk in the Science lab.

# Cognition and learning

This category of needs may include students who demonstrate moderate or severe learning difficulties, or more specific difficulties, such as dyslexia or dyspraxia. These students benefit from specific programmes to help cognition and learning. It may include some students on the autistic spectrum.

| Split things up into small steps | • Put practical instructions on cards to carry out in order.<br><br>• Split the stages in a process into separate steps. For example, this could work well to understand negative feedback or the carbon cycle.<br><br>• Design learning activities so students work through distinct steps with concise and explicit instructions.<br><br>• Give lessons clear structure, so students know what they are going to do right from the start of the lesson.<br><br>• Think about questions in advance. Focus each question on one concept, rather than expecting students to provide answers which integrate different concepts immediately. |
|---|---|

→

| Help students to engage with text, and seek alternatives where possible | • Use a sans-serif font on worksheets (e.g. Helvetica or Arial) and space writing and pictures out on the page.<br><br>• Use numbered points in text on a whiteboard to help students pick out different ideas.<br><br>• Use coloured paper rather than white paper, and a coloured background on the whiteboard, to reduce glare from incident sunlight, and make reading easier.<br><br>• Use a variety of approaches to communicating ideas, such as videos, apps and audio recordings to help students to learn. |
|---|---|
| Help students to process information | • Design practical instructions so it is clear where the instructions are telling students (a) what they have to **do,** (b) what they need to **think about** and (c) what and where they have to **write.**<br><br>• Before starting a practical activity, ask students to explain in their own words what they are going to do. |
| Provide support with abstract ideas and scientific vocabulary | • Focus on the meanings of technical words to help develop students' understanding of the concept.<br><br>• Start by exploring scientific phenomena in everyday contexts before discussing abstract ideas. For example, ask students to make a lamp light with a battery and wires before discussing electric current.<br><br>• When everyday contexts are impossible to find, use other strategies such as modelling, drama, simulation and role play to help develop concepts in students' minds.<br><br>• Focus on one concept at a time, rather than trying to introduce several concepts at once. |
| Activate peers as learning resources for each other | • Use small group work to enable students to learn at their own pace while receiving support from each other. |

**Table 10.4:** Cognition and learning strategies.

🖸 **LESSON IDEA ONLINE 10.3: TEACHING THROUGH EVERYDAY CONTEXTS**

Think about how students will have encountered a scientific phenomenon in their everyday lives, as this can help you to think of useful contexts around which to frame a lesson. Use an inquiry question to help students think through the ideas in context.

# Sensory, physical and medical needs

This category of needs includes a wide spectrum of multi–sensory, physical and medical difficulties. These may include hearing loss or visual impairment. Physical impairments may simply be physically disabling, while some conditions may also lead to complex learning and social needs. Sensory, physical or medical needs do not necessarily mean a student will have additional educational needs.

| | |
|---|---|
| **Physical access** | • Ensure there is sufficient space for wheelchair users to move around the laboratory, especially during practical. |
| | • Consider installing height-adjustable laboratory benches, with sufficient space underneath for a wheelchair (Figure 10.1). |
| | • The laboratory entrances should be ramped if necessary. |
| | • Position laboratory equipment at wheelchair height. |
| **Auditory access** | • Think about the effects of background noise during practical work. Seat hearing-impaired students with other students in the more silent part of the laboratory. |
| | • If using a microphone amplification system, remember to turn it off before raising your voice to gain attention. |
| | • Ensure you do not stand in front of a strong light source, as it can stop students lip-reading. |
| **Visual access** | • Use microscope cameras to magnify microscope images to TV or PC. |
| | • Employ magnifiers to help students read textbooks, or use e-textbooks with adjustable font size. |
| | • Introduce teaching assistants to laboratory equipment so they can support students' practical work. |
| | • Where possible, convert learning resources into Braille versions. |

→

| Access to learning activities | <ul><li>Amend your programme of study to ensure learning activities are achievable by students with sensory, physical or medical needs in your class. For example, students with brittle bones will not be able to undertake physical activity in an investigation on heart rate; students may be unable to stand for long periods, affecting their ability to do practical work.</li><li>Ensure academic demands are not based on physical ability.</li><li>Seek specialist advice from the special needs coordinator and other professionals where appropriate.</li><li>Employ ICT to support investigative work. For example, provide blank writing frames, pre-created tables to record data, or data-logging software for students lacking fine motor control.</li></ul> |
|---|---|

**Table 10.5:** Providing access.

**Figure 10.1:** Wheelchair-accessible laboratory bench.

Teacher Tip

If you have a learning support assistant, provide them with a copy of your programme of study and lesson plan in advance each week, so they can think about how to support students' learning with special needs.

Teacher Tip

Do you have a seating plan for your lesson? If so, is it designed to best support students with special educational needs who need additional support? Think about how to seat students so they don't feel separate, but so their needs are best provided for. For example, you may put a student in a wheelchair close to the exit.

**Summary**

- Create an inclusive classroom to support all students' learning, whether or not they have special needs.

- Think about differentiation when lesson planning, designing lesson activities to enable all students to learn.

- Know your students, and make adaptations to overcome their particular barriers to learning.

# Teaching with digital technologies

**11**

# What are digital technologies?

Digital technologies enable our students to access a wealth of up-to-date digital resources, collaborate locally and globally, curate existing material and create new material. They include electronic devices and tools that manage and manipulate information and data.

# Why use digital technologies in the classroom?

When used successfully, digital technologies have the potential to transform teaching and learning. The effective use of technology in the classroom encourages active learning, knowledge construction, inquiry and exploration among students. It should enhance an existing task or provide opportunities to do things that could not be done without it. It can also enhance the role of assessment, providing new ways for students to demonstrate evidence of learning.

New technologies are redefining relationships and enabling new opportunities. But there are also risks, so we should encourage our students to be knowledgeable about and responsible in their use of technology. Integrating technology into our teaching helps prepare students for a future rooted in an increasingly digitised world.

# What are the challenges of using digital technologies?

The key to ensuring that technology is used effectively is to remember that it is simply a resource, and not an end in itself. As with the use of all resources, the key is not to start with the resource itself, but to start with what you want the student to learn. We need to think carefully about why and how to use technologies as well as evaluating their efficiency and effectiveness.

If students are asked to use digital technologies as part of their homework, it is important that all students are able to access the relevant technology outside school. A school needs to think about a response to any 'digital divide', because if technology is 'adding value', then all students need to be able to benefit. Some schools choose to make resources available to borrow or use in school, or even loan devices to students.

Safety for students and teachers is a key challenge for schools and it is important to consider issues such as the prevention of cyber-bullying, the hacking of personal information, access to illegal or banned materials and distractions from learning. As technology changes, schools and teachers need to adapt and implement policies and rules.

One of the greatest pitfalls is for a teacher to feel that they are not skilled technologists, and therefore not to try. Creative things can be done with simple technology, and a highly effective teacher who knows very little about technology can often achieve much more than a less effective teacher who is a technology expert. Knowing how to use technology is not the same as knowing how to teach with it.

# Decide on the learning, *then* choose the technology

As new technologies become cheaper and more easily available, the choice as to what we might use will only get harder. It is easy to think that the next new technology will transform your teaching, but you will always remain the most important thing in the room. In his 1980 book, *Electronic Tutors*, Arthur C Clarke wrote: 'Any teacher that can be replaced by a machine should be!' We should remember this when we see the latest technological tool that promises to transform our classrooms.

This chapter will look at the opportunities that can make a difference. However, we always need to begin with decisions about teaching and learning, then look for technological solutions, not the other way around.

# The digital filing cabinet

Many schools have shelves and cupboards full of resources that have been accumulated over many years, some used regularly, others easily forgotten. Find time to collate, organise (and scan if needed) all the things you have into one place. Think carefully about how you name and arrange things to make it easier for others to search and find things. You might consider some or all of the following:

- collections of professional and teaching materials to share among colleagues
- material from lessons for students who need to catch up
- supplementary resources for keen and committed students
- homework and follow-up materials (can also be shared with parents).

Many networks and cloud storage systems allow you to control access, but be careful: you may want to share homework, but you don't want to let the students see the test answers!

---

**Teacher Tip**

Collect your five favourite digital resources (e.g. a website or a video clip) and share them via email or a network drive with at least one of your colleagues, asking them to do the same. You'll soon have an impressive collection.

---

# Every picture tells a story

When learning Science, diagrams can be valuable and useful, but sometimes drawing them can be time-consuming and challenging for some students, distracting them from the Science ideas we want to focus on. Digital cameras are cheap, readily available and can capture and share images instantly. Lesson ideas 11.1–11.3 will give you some things to try straight away and hopefully inspire you to come up with more ideas. Make sure you keep a copy of the best work and photos to share and use again.

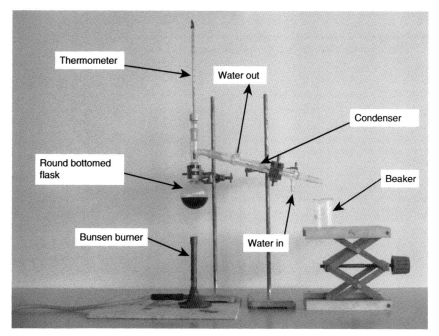

**Figure 11.1:** Labelled photo of a distillation apparatus.

## LESSON IDEA 11.1: INSTANT DIAGRAM

The next time you ask students to carry out an experiment with complex equipment (e.g. distillation or electrolysis), rather than asking them to draw a diagram, get them to take a photo of the equipment, print it out and label it.

## ☑ LESSON IDEA ONLINE 11.2: MITOSIS AND MEIOSIS ANIMATED

When learning about dynamic multi-stage processes (e.g. mitosis and meiosis or embryo development), students make a model or draw diagrams for each stage. They photograph each stage in turn and use photo/video software to make a slide show or animation showing the whole process. Most video software will allow them to record and add an audio soundtrack to explain the process. See Lesson idea 11.2 for more details.

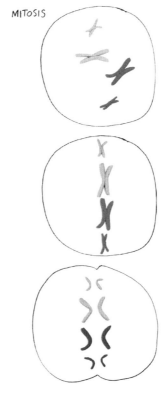

**Figure 11.2:** Some stages from a student's stop frame animation of mitosis.

## ☑ LESSON IDEA ONLINE 11.3: ANNOTATE REAL LIFE

When teaching gravity and air resistance, ask students to drop an object such as a cupcake case and take photo(s) of it in motion. The students then annotate these photo(s) showing the size and direction of the forces acting, helping them to connect the real world (falling object) with the abstract one (forces you cannot 'see'). Magnetic fields and electric currents also provide opportunities in this regard. See Lesson idea 11.3 for more details.

**Figure 11.3:** Annotated photos illustrating gravity.

Starting with photos makes it easier to work stage-by-stage and delete any individual mistakes without having to start from the beginning. Once you feel confident with photos, you can move on to video!

# Using technology to capture data

The collection of data is a regular part of Science lessons. In addition to stand-alone datalogging equipment, many teachers and students carry a datalogger with them all the time, on their smartphones. Datalogging should not replace students collecting results themselves, but sometimes things happen too quickly (e.g. collisions between moving objects) or too slowly (e.g. seed germination) to make it easy to collect data by hand. In other situations, schools may not have the equipment that is inside a smartphone (e.g. magnetic field sensor, accelerometer). Table 11.1 lists some common smartphone sensors you could use in addition to or instead of stand–alone dataloggers.

**Teacher Tip**

Many smartphones don't automatically show readings from these sensors. There are lots of free apps that can do this.

| Smartphone feature/sensor | Opportunities to use in Science teaching |
|---|---|
| Time lapse photographs | Seed germination, action of yeast, oxidation of fruit, phototropism, ice melting on different thermal conductors, displacement reactions. *Note: make sure you pick an appropriate time interval.* |
| Accelerometer | Measuring the acceleration of a falling object (drop it on something soft!) or on a roller coaster to see the changes in acceleration. Use the three accelerometers in most phones to show how a seismometer works. |
| Light meter | Measure changes in light intensity with distance, the behaviour of a light-dependent-resistor, light transmission through solutions. |
| GPS | During field work, take photos and GPS-tag their location. You could add them to a digital map later. |

**Table 11.1:** Smartphone features and their possible uses in class.

**Teacher Tip**

You may need to calibrate the sensors on your phone to get accurate measurements so check the settings in the app/ phone. Even if you don't do this, you'll be able to see and compare changes between readings.

Don't forget the camera on a smartphone. Some have a zoom that turns them into a pocket microscope and, if connected to a data-projector, you have an instant visualizer and students won't have to crowd around the front desk.

# Using technology to process and present data

Once students have collected data, they need to process it, which often involves calculations and graph drawing. Both are important skills that students need to develop and technology should never totally replace them, but if we have limited time in class then we can use the technology available to allow us to focus on the most important parts of the lesson.

Spreadsheets can be used to process large data sets; they can work out averages or carry out multi-step calculations. Students can put experimental data into a pre-prepared spreadsheet and instantly get processed data. Spreadsheets can also be set up to automatically draw graphs of data so students can see patterns emerging as data is inputted.

## Teacher Tip

If the students are not used to using spreadsheets in this way, you can prepare one in advance to do the calculations (and draw graphs) automatically. As students become more confident, they can set up the spreadsheets themselves or you can deliberately make errors for them to find.

## ☑ LESSON IDEA ONLINE 11.4: RADIOACTIVE DICE

When teaching radioactive decay and half-life, this can be modelled using six-sided dice. Students get a set of around 100 dice, throw them all, remove any with a six and then repeat until they have no more, recording how many remained after each throw. They put this data into a spreadsheet that can be set to draw a graph of the results. You can also have a spreadsheet that combines the whole class's results. Figure 11.4 shows what this might look like. See Lesson idea 11.4 for more details.

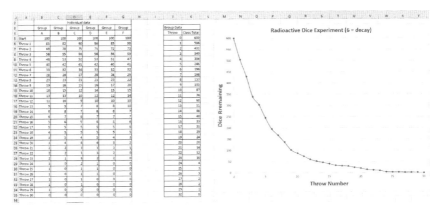

**Figure 11.4:** Spreadsheet and graph of a radioactive dice experiment.

---

### Teacher Tip

Tracker is a piece of software that will analyse video of any moving object. It is available free on the internet and will give you motion data and graphs for anything you film.

There are also smartphone/tablet apps available that do similar things.

---

# Flipped learning

Flipped learning uses technology to get the students to prepare for the lesson (by watching a short video clip, for example), which allows more time in class for discussions, questions and activities. The name 'flipped' (i.e. turned over) comes from this changing of the more usual order of the directly taught part of the lesson and the follow-up activities.

There is no right way to run a flipped lesson. The key idea is that the students have seen and thought about some of the ideas in the lesson beforehand. As well as choosing the right video, you need to plan to make the best use of the extra time you have made in the lesson. Eric Mazur from Harvard University starts with a question based on the key ideas, students answer it on their own, then discuss their answers in groups and do the question again. This approach, where the discussion between students supports learning, is called **Peer Instruction**. More details are in Mazur's book of the same name.

---

### LESSON IDEA 11.5: USING VIDEOS

For an upcoming lesson, pick one video you think will help students prepare. Set this as homework and change your lesson plan to follow the peer instruction model.

---

## Why is flipped learning worth trying?

When presented with new information, students must listen, take notes and process these ideas at the same time. Having prior knowledge of a topic, even if incomplete, can help. If the students watch the video beforehand, the learning starts before the lesson begins.

You may want to begin by using freely available videos, eventually making your own or even getting the class to make some. The latter is also a great way to test students' understanding. You need to pick lessons where the content can be clearly explained in a video, and think about what to do if students haven't watched it; but the only way to find out what works is to try it out yourself.

# Simulations and visualisation

Science studies the word around us, but much of what we study is hard to see because it is too small or large (e.g. bacteria and galaxies) or happens too quickly or too slowly (e.g. some chemical reactions and evolution). There are many interactive simulations available in apps, software or web pages that allow us to observe scientific processes that are beyond our senses. We can speed things up, slow them down, zoom in and out and change variables that we would not be able to change otherwise. Table 11.2 lists some readily available visualisations and simulations.

| Science topic/ideas | Notes | Benefit/Value |
|---|---|---|
| Motion graphs | A moving object and its corresponding motion graph(s) are drawn in real time. | Helps students connect static graphs to dynamic motions. |
| Electric circuits | Students build, test and take measurement from virtual circuits. | Can avoid challenges with sometimes unreliable equipment. |
| Electrolysis | Students change solutions and potential difference, observing effects. | Allows students to visualise and connect macroscopic and microscopic behaviour (e.g. gas production and ion movement). |
| Reactions and rates | Students change initial concentrations of reactants and see final products, measuring rate. | Allows students to carry out reactions not possible in class because of safety, equipment or timescale limitations. |
| Populations (predator/ prey) | Example: foxes and rabbits game where you vary the initial amount of either of these and see how the populations change over time. | Allows visualising of how dynamic relationships change and how initial conditions influence final outcome. |

**Table 11.2:** Visualisations and simulations.

Interactive simulations should not replace real observation and practical work, but they can show complex dynamic and microscopic processes that students cannot normally see, as well as allowing them to ask and answer 'what if?' questions that they couldn't do in class.

---

Teacher Tip

The PhET site is one of the best free Science simulation websites. It is focused on Physics but has some Biology and Chemistry content.

---

# Working together

Science is a collaborative activity whereby multiple scientists work together to collect data, publish and share new ideas. We can replicate this in class by using wikis. A wiki is a website that can be edited by more than one person. Rather than asking for written work, you can get individuals or groups to collaborate, producing their work on wiki pages.

---

Teacher Tip

There are many websites where you can set up a wiki for your class quickly, easily and for free. Wikispaces and PBworks are two sites commonly used in education. You can set up class accounts and track activity; this can help you to monitor individual progress.

---

## LESSON IDEA 11.6: SUMMARISING TOPICS

At the end of a topic, give each member of the class (or group) a topic and ask them to write a revision wiki page. When complete, students can edit/revise/comment on another page.

Using a wiki allows students to edit and change their work as they go along, as well as add content or comments to each other's work, building a supportive, collaborative environment in class.

# Online professional development

In a busy school, it is easy to focus all your energies on your lessons and the students, but it is important to find time to reflect on your own personal development and look for ways to develop and improve your practice.

---

**Teacher Tip**

STEM Learning, based in the UK, is one of the most comprehensive sources of resources and advice for Science teachers anywhere. There is a large electronic library as well as special interest forums and groups you can join.

---

As well as finding other teachers sharing classroom materials, search for blogs and sites where teachers reflect on their own teaching and talk about new strategies and approaches that they are trying. There are also online professional development courses, some of which are free to join. Most of these sites encourage comment and questions so don't be passive – join in the discussions. The nature of these sites means that you can engage at times which suit you and connect with like-minded teachers all over the globe. They may be facing many of the same challenges as you and have some good suggestions as to what you might try.

---

**Teacher Tip**

There are many excellent resources available on the internet. However, there are also resources, blogs and other materials that may be inappropriate for your context or contain factual errors. Look for sites supported by organisations that you know or that show feedback from other users. You could also ask a colleague to check materials to help you find the best of what is available.

---

Connecting with other professionals, sharing ideas and experiences helps to make us feel supported and valued outside our school. This can only be a good thing. At the same time, we develop and grow as professionals.

**Summary**

Digital technologies can provide fantastic opportunities and experiences. Remember, though, that they are just a tool; we should start with the learning and **then** pick the tool that might help. Some of the main ways in which we can use digital technologies in Science teaching are:

- Capturing and processing data – Use dataloggers and sensors to collect experimental data and cameras to record observations. Use spreadsheets to process and present data.

- Communicating and sharing – Before the lesson, resources can help students prepare for lessons (flipped learning) and after the lesson you can share homework and students can collaborate.

- See the unseen – Visualisation of objects and processes that we cannot see.

- Professional development – Resources and opportunities to help us become better teachers.

# 12 | Global thinking

# What is global thinking?

Global thinking is about learning how to live in a complex world as an active and engaged citizen. It is about considering the bigger picture and appreciating the nature and depth of our shared humanity.

When we encourage global thinking in students we help them recognise, examine and express their own and others' perspectives. We need to scaffold students' thinking to enable them to engage on cognitive, social and emotional levels, and construct their understanding of the world to be able to participate fully in its future.

We as teachers can help students develop routines and habits of mind to enable them to move beyond the familiar, discern that which is of local and global significance, make comparisons, take a cultural perspective and challenge stereotypes. We can encourage them to learn about contexts and traditions, and provide opportunities for them to reflect on their own and others' viewpoints.

# Why adopt a global thinking approach?

Global thinking is particularly relevant in an interconnected, digitised world where ideas, opinions and trends are rapidly and relentlessly circulated. Students learn to pause and evaluate. They study why a topic is important on a personal, local and global scale, and they will be motivated to understand the world and their significance in it. Students gain a deeper understanding of why different viewpoints and ideas are held across the world.

Global thinking is something we can nurture both within and across disciplines. We can invite students to learn how to use different lenses from each discipline to see and interpret the world. They also learn how best to apply and communicate key concepts within and across disciplines. We can help our students select the appropriate media and technology to communicate and create their own personal synthesis of the information they have gathered.

Global thinking enables students to become more rounded individuals who perceive themselves as actors in a global context and who value diversity. It encourages them to become more aware, curious and interested in learning about the world and how it works. It helps students to challenge assumptions and stereotypes, to be better informed and more respectful. Global thinking takes the focus beyond exams and grades, or even checklists of skills and attributes. It develops students who are more ready to compete in the global marketplace and more able to participate effectively in an interconnected world.

# What are the challenges of incorporating global thinking?

The pressures of an already full curriculum, the need to meet national and local standards, and the demands of exam preparation may make it seem challenging to find time to incorporate global thinking into lessons and programmes of study. A whole-school approach may be required for global thinking to be incorporated in subject plans for teaching and learning.

We need to give all students the opportunity to find their voice and participate actively and confidently, regardless of their background and world experiences, when exploring issues of global significance. We need to design suitable activities that are clear, ongoing and varying. Students need to be able to connect with materials, and extend and challenge their thinking. We also need to devise and use new forms of assessment that incorporate flexible and cooperative thinking.

# Global thinking in Science

In the Science classroom, we have a lot of opportunities to help students think globally. Wouldn't it be fantastic if your students could deconstruct, analyse and evaluate something that someone says in the newspapers? And wouldn't it be equally good if they could build their own point of view, researching, identifying and evaluating the evidence for opposite sides of the argument? Finally, they should be able to reflect upon what this means for their own opinions, and then communicate their thinking, using the evidence they gained, both individually and collaboratively. The skills identified in this paragraph include skills students need for global thinking:

- collaboration
- critical thinking and problem solving
- independent research
- communication
- reflection
- innovation and creative thinking.

Many of these ideas have already been considered in this book. For example, in Chapter 6 **Active learning**, we looked at collaboration through group work, and at inquiry, which fosters critical thinking and creativity in identifying hypotheses and devising approaches to testing them. Although we may provide lots of opportunity to **rehearse** these kinds of thinking, by thinking about them when we plan our lessons, we can use Science teaching to help students to **learn and develop** these types of thinking. In this chapter, you will learn about some approaches, which can enable students both to learn the Science, but also to engage in and develop their global thinking.

## Teacher Tip

Using news media in your teaching can be helpful in developing students' critical thinking. Identifying bias and inaccuracy in the reporting of scientific ideas can provide a springboard both for learning the 'correct' Science, but also for developing students' critical thinking skills.

# Thinking about controversial issues

In Science, there are a number of controversial issues which are at a global scale and which students need to approach using 'global thinking' in order to make sense of them. This could involve questions around nuclear power, evolution by natural selection or climate change. So how can you develop students' global thinking by considering controversial issues?

---

Teacher Tip

In some countries, you may need to reflect upon whether a particular controversial issue should be discussed in the classroom. Seek advice from your senior leadership team if necessary.

---

First, teach any non-controversial scientific knowledge linked to the issue, or allow students to conduct their own research to find out about it. Second, use activities that enable students to reflect on the controversy. These may include activities that draw upon role play, debate or drama. By adopting 'characters', it is easier for students to reflect objectively, without feelings impacting upon their reflections. For example:

- **Balloon debate.** Four or five characters, for example with different views of evolution by natural selection, justify why they should not be thrown out of a balloon; audience evaluates and makes the decision.
- **TV chat show.** Four or five characters take part in a mock TV chat show, for example, about global warming.
- **Improvised drama.** Students improvise a short drama about a dilemma. The dilemma is related to the controversy; the drama is

improvised after characters have been briefed. For example, the dilemma may be about whether to have a genetic test.

- **Hot seating.** Each character sits on a chair in front of the audience; the audience debates with the character rather than the individual. This can work particularly well for debates about genetically modified food.

- **Advocates.** Main character faced with a dilemma related to the controversy. Two other students play 'advocates', who argue the case from opposite points of view. For example, the character may be a mother deciding whether to have a 'saviour sibling' to generate bone marrow for her ill son. The advocates present opposing arguments to influence her decision.

- **Mantle of the expert**. Individuals take on the role of experts, for example as scientists, nuclear power employees or environmental campaigners. Rather than simply 'role-playing' under a teacher's direction, they actually behave and think like experts. For example, one may take on the role of designer of a zoo, and another the role of education officer. Each will decide upon the key features of their role, and undertake key tasks, such as design of enclosures, or design of education materials. Mantle of the expert always involves an 'enterprise' which the students are involved in 'running', with as much involvement and commitment as if the enterprise was real. The teacher may need to supply information, or give students the chance to do research into their allocated roles.

**Figure 12.1:** A lively debate in class.

Having run one of the activities, ask students to identify the goals, rights and responsibilities of the different characters involved in the controversy. They should think what the controversy is about: values, information or concepts? They should then identify the key questions that lie at the heart of the issue. These questions can be divided into:

- Questions relating to values: What should be? What is best?
- Questions relating to information: What is the truth? What are the facts?
- Questions relating to concepts: What does this mean? How should this be defined?

Then consider:

1   What are the arguments? This is an analytical step in which students carefully consider what is presented by both sides of the issue. Have students write down or 'paraphrase' the arguments that are presented. Most controversial issues arise because of differing values, so it is useful for students to identify the set of values that underlie the argument. Can they differentiate between personal opinions and more informed points of view?

2   What are the assumptions behind the argument? What is taken as self-evident in the presentation of the argument? Students might then apply their own principles to help them determine the validity of a position – in other words, if students decide that the assumptions are unethical or unprincipled, it reduces the strength of the argument.

3   How are the arguments manipulated? This step is particularly important because it can help students understand how information can be used to influence opinion. What information has been addressed, selected, emphasised or ignored according to its value to different positions on an issue?

Finally, help students to find a solution to the controversy. Bear in mind that there should be no obligation for students to change their personal views about the controversy. However, having been through Steps 1–3, students may need to find a new solution that reflects their analysis of the issue.

---

### Teacher Tip

Look back at the activities listed at the start of this section. Think about where each component of global thinking comes into the process. Don't forget that you need to draw out the conceptual learning too, depending on the topic – not just the global thinking.

---

Students think about and record the consequences of a decision which is influenced by scientific knowledge, engaging with that knowledge in the process.

# Argumentation and inquiry

Controversial issues like this can be used to build students' argumentation skills. Although we hope that students will be able to analyse and build arguments, we do need to help them. There are two useful ways to look at argument. Toulmin wrote about the components of an argument, which you can see in Table 12.1.

| | |
|---|---|
| **Claim**<br><br>*A statement which you want someone to accept* | Blond-haired people are taller. |
| **Data**<br><br>*The evidence upon which the claim is based* | Mean height of blond-haired people, and mean height of non-blond-haired people. |
| **Warrant**<br><br>*Links data with the claim* | *Because* mean height of blond-haired people is higher, blond-haired people are taller. |
| **Backing**<br><br>*Support for the argument, which may come from asking different questions* | Scandinavian countries (with lots of blond-haired people) have a higher proportion of tall people. |
| **Qualifiers and reservations**<br><br>*Indicates the strength of the connection from the data to the warrant, and may limit how universal the claim is* | Blond-haired people are *likely* to be taller than other people.<br><br>*Most* blond-haired people are taller than other people. |
| **Rebuttal**<br><br>*The rebuttal of a counter-claim* | A counter-argument could challenge the claim, if the sampling of people was not random. A rebuttal would deny this, asserting that sampling was random. |

**Table 12.1:** Toulmin's framework for argument.

We can support students' argumentation skills by providing a writing frame to help them. Figure 12.2 provides an example. Asking students to write up inquiry work using a frame like this helps them to focus on evidence, theories and explanations, building an understanding of the nature of evidence.

---

### LESSON IDEA 12.3: USING THE ARGUMENT WRITING FRAME

Use the argument writing frame (Figure 12.2) in one of your practical lessons. Reflect with students on what goes in each box, and explicitly point out the steps they have gone through in building their argument.

---

## Building an argument

**Figure 12.2:** An argument writing frame.

There are other approaches to building arguments too. Walton in 1996 identified different types of arguments:

- **Argument from sign.** An observation is taken as evidence of an event. For example, there are bear tracks in the snow, so a bear was here.
- **Argument from example.** If something has a property, then it will also have another property. For example, if something is magnetic, then it will be hard and shiny.
- **Argument from commitment.** Because someone has a particular property, someone expects them to be committed to a position. For example, if somebody is a large-scale farmer, making money from agriculture, they may be expected to support genetic modification of crops.
- **Argument from cause to effect.** If one type of event occurs, it is predicted that another event will occur. For example, because the tube was heated, the bubbles were released more quickly.

You can make use of the arguments above in lessons too. Often they'll feature in your own explanations of scientific phenomena. Or you may use one of these to help students build a hypothesis. Think about where in your explanations you use these kinds of argument.

# Making ethical decisions

The following types of argument may be useful when students are faced with socio-scientific issues which involve ethical decisions, rather than just scientific data. These could include decisions about whether to use nuclear power, whether a child should be vaccinated, or whether genetic modification of food is right. If you help students to understand the ethical issues, then they can construct arguments to help separate the Science from the ethics. There are two main approaches students take in making ethical decisions:

- **Non-consequentialism.** An act is right or wrong, just because of the act itself. For example, it is wrong to murder. Some students may feel it is wrong to manipulate genes, and so genetic modification of food and gene therapy are wrong.
- **Consequentialism.** An act is right or wrong, depending on how much 'good' results from it. The more good consequences there are, the more right is the act. Because of this, a person should choose the action that maximises good consequences. On this basis, someone

would support genetic modification of food (because it helps maximise yield) and gene therapy (because it cures disease).

When you try to work on a particular topic, you may find students have strong views about the topic itself. For example, some students may be so firm that genetic engineering is wrong, they will be unable to think critically about it, or to learn from an activity that uses an ethical debate to help them to learn. It is important to give their opinions value. However, ask them to explain the basis for their view, so they realise when they are making a decision based on what they think is right or wrong, or whether they are making a decision based on consequences.

# Problem-solving and practical learning

Setting problems for students to solve can work really well:

- to ask students to apply their knowledge
- to help students to learn conceptual ideas
- to help students to build up their global thinking skills.

There are lots of examples, but let's think about a task where students are asked to get a small ball from a table top to the floor as slowly as possible. It doesn't sound very scientific, but think again. Students can apply knowledge about friction (in trying to slow the ball down), rotational movement (if they make the ball spin round and round down a tube) and levers (if the ball triggers a set of levers on the way).

They can also see these phenomena first hand without knowing anything about them, and build up their own questions about them. Not only does it trigger their creativity in thinking up the questions, but it also allows them to feel more ownership of their learning because they came up with the questions and hypotheses. Of course, the problems you set will be 'pre-programmed' to trigger students' ideas in particular directions, but when they investigate their own hypothesis, they are more engaged and more likely to learn.

In a challenge like this, students go through a process of planning, designing, making, testing and refining. It doesn't even have to be an explicit problem. For example, they may just be asked to make a set of gears. While they are making them, they practise communication and collaboration by working on it with others. They reflect on success and failure as they try new approaches. And they are stimulated to think creatively as they think up new approaches.

Once students are involved in a task like this, it becomes very absorbing and builds a momentum from which ideas are created. In testing different ideas, students set smaller goals, working towards the final goal, based on their own strengths and limitations. For the ball problem, this is obvious. Each goal is set by students to try to slow the ball down a little bit more. But for the gears, they may think of their own directions to set – for example, they may try to make the gears work more smoothly, drive more cogs and so on.

If you employ a task like this, you can really support students' thinking. The kinds of thinking skills this activity can build are included in Table 12.2. You should be able to see that these include many of the skills required for global thinking, which we talked about earlier.

| Creativity and divergent thinking | Using a wide range of idea creation techniques, for example planning, sketching, brainstorming. |
|---|---|
| | Developing unique strategies, tools, objects or outcomes. |
| | Creating new ways to use materials or tools. |
| | Setting personal long- and short-term goals and planning ways to achieve these. |
| Ingenuity, inventiveness and innovation | Using or modifying others' ideas or strategies to create something new. |
| | Demonstrating originality and inventiveness. |
| | Understanding and experiencing real world limits to new ideas and goals. |
| | Coming up with novel solutions and possibilities when faced with problems or obstacles. |
| Communication and collaboration | Incorporating input and feedback from other people (e.g. peers or a facilitator) into their work. |
| | Developing, implementing and communicating new ideas to others effectively. |
| | Being open and responsive to new and diverse ideas. |

→

| Problem solving, critical thinking and reflection | Posing problems to solve. |
|---|---|
| | Identifying emerging problems. |
| | Coming up with solutions or methods to try to find solutions. |
| | Elaborating, refining, analysing, testing and evaluating ideas. |
| | Planning steps for future action. |
| | Striving to understand, for example exploring confusion and/or obstacles to build new understanding. |
| | Connecting to prior knowledge, including STEM concepts. |
| | Employing what has been learnt during explorations. |
| | Complexifying thinking and understanding by engaging in increasingly complicated and sophisticated work. |
| Resilience and risk-taking | Persisting to optimise strategies or solutions. |
| | Viewing failure as an opportunity to learn: getting stuck and working to become unstuck. |
| | Trying something new or never (personally) attempted before. |
| | Trying something where there is a lack of confidence in outcome. |
| | Becoming comfortable with a process of small successes and frequent mistakes. |
| | Persisting toward a goal in the face of setbacks or frustration. |

**Table 12.2:** Skills developed through engaging in problem-solving, making and tinkering activities (Adapted from *Tinkering: A Practitioner Guide for Developing and Implementing Tinkering Activities*, available online on the Museo Nazionale della Scienza e della Tecnologia Leonardo da Vinci website).

To design activities like this, which foster the skills for global thinking, you should keep five criteria in mind:

- Make it personal, physical, immersive and creative. Students should be choosing their own materials and playing around with them.
- Make sure it involves students designing a solution, which then makes them think of another refinement, or another problem, which

then needs another design. For example, students may find one solution to get the ball to the floor, but implementing it may help them to think about a different solution.

- Ensure students work together so they can get help from each other, and create an atmosphere where they feel able to ask you for help as the teacher (but don't give them solutions; ask them questions to help them come up with their own solutions).
- Arrange the lab space to maximise interaction and collaboration. For example, you could even spread the resources around the room so they can pick up ideas from each other when they go to collect them.

## LESSON IDEA 12.4: FOSTERING GLOBAL THINKING

Think up a similar activity that builds upon something you teach, but that also fulfils many of the five criteria used to foster skills for global thinking. Having designed it, write down what your learning objectives are, both conceptually and for students' thinking skills.

Your own ideas for these kinds of activities will usually come from what you are teaching. Here are two examples relevant to Physics teaching that can build the skills needed for global thinking:

- Create and build a vehicle that must move, but without a battery
- Take a motorised toy apart to find out how it works, but make sure it still works at the end.

Teacher Tip

Don't make these kinds of activities into a competition. It discourages diverse thinking.

**Summary**

- Global thinking is not something extra; it is very much part of Science. But it is important to plan for global thinking, rather than just expecting it to happen.

- Global thinking can be planned for, and practised by students through:

  (a) thinking about controversial issues; useful strategies include drama and questioning to engage with the issues effectively

  (b) thinking about and making arguments

  (c) thinking about ethics, understanding whether things are right or wrong, or whether they have good or bad effects

  (d) problem-solving, tinkering and making; approaches which foster creativity, innovation, communication, collaboration and problem-solving skills.

# Reflective practice

## 13

Dr Paul Beedle, Head of Professional Development Qualifications, Cambridge International Examinations

# 13 Approaches to learning and teaching Science

## *'As a teacher you are always learning'*

It is easy to say this, isn't it? Is it true? Are you bound to learn just by being a teacher?

You can learn every day from the experience of working with your students, collaborating with your colleagues and playing your part in the life of your school. You can learn also by being receptive to new ideas and approaches, and by applying and evaluating these in practice in your own context.

To be more precise, let us say that as a teacher:

- You **should** always be learning
  to develop your expertise throughout your career for your own fulfilment as a member of the teaching profession and to be as effective as possible in the classroom
- You **can** always be learning
  if you approach the teaching experience with an open mind, ready to learn and knowing how to reflect on what you are doing in order to improve.

You want your professional development activities to be as relevant as possible to what you do and who you are, and to help change the quality of your teaching and your students' learning – for the better, in terms of outcomes, and for good, in terms of lasting effect. You want to feel that 'it all makes sense' and that you are actively following a path that works for you personally, professionally and career-wise.

So professional learning is about making the most of opportunities and your working environment, bearing in mind who you are, what you are like and how you want to improve. But simply experiencing – thinking about and responding to situations, and absorbing ideas and information – is not necessarily learning. It is through reflection that you can make the most of your experience to deepen and extend your professional skills and understanding.

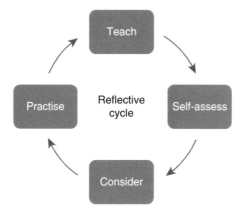

**Figure 13.1:** Reflective practice.

In this chapter, we will focus on three *essentials* of reflective practice, explaining in principle and in practice how you can support your own continuing professional development:

1  **Focusing** on what you want to learn about and why
2  **Challenging** yourself and others to go beyond description and assumptions to critical analysis and evaluation
3  **Sharing** what you are learning with colleagues – to enrich understanding and enhance the quality of practice.

These essentials will help you as you apply and adapt the rich ideas and approaches in this book in your own particular context. They will also help you if you are, or are about to be, taking part in a Cambridge Professional Development Qualification (Cambridge PDQ) programme, to make the most of your programme, develop your portfolio and gain the qualification.

## 1  Focus
*In principle*

Given the multiple dimensions and demands of being a teacher, you might be tempted to try to cover 'everything' in your professional development but you will then not have the time to go beneath the surface much at all. Likewise, attending many different training events will certainly keep you very busy but it is unlikely that these will simply add up to improving your thinking and practice in sustainable and systematic ways.

Teachers who are beginning an organised programme of professional learning find that it is most helpful to select particular ideas, approaches and topics which are relevant to their own situation and their school's priorities. They can then be clear about their professional learning goals, and how their own learning contributes to improving their students' learning outcomes. They deliberately choose activities that help make sense of their practice with their students in their school and have clear overall purpose.

It is one thing achieving focus, and another maintaining this over time. When the going gets tough, because it is difficult either to understand or become familiar with new ideas and practices, or to balance learning time with the demands of work and life, it really helps to have a mission – to know why you want to learn something as well as what that something is. Make sure that this is a purpose which you feel genuinely belongs to you and in which you have a keen interest, rather than it being something given to you or imposed on you. Articulate your focus not just by writing it down but by 'pitching' it to a colleague whose opinion you trust and taking note of their feedback.

*In practice*

- Plan
  *What is my goal and how will I approach the activity?*

  Select an approach that is new to you, but make sure that you understand the thinking behind this and that it is relevant to your students' learning. Do it for real effect, not for show.

- Monitor
  *Am I making progress towards my goal; do I need to try a different approach?*

  Take time during your professional development programme to review how far and well you are developing your understanding of theory and practice. What can you do to get more out of the experience, for example by discussing issues with your mentor, researching particular points, and asking your colleagues for their advice?

- Evaluate
  *What went well, what could have been better, what have I learnt for next time?*

  Evaluation can sometimes be seen as a 'duty to perform' – like clearing up after the event – rather than the pivotal moment in learning that it really is. Evaluate not because you are told you have to; evaluate to make sense of the learning experience you have been through and what it means to you, and to plan ahead to see what you can do in the future.

This cycle of planning, monitoring and evaluation is just as relevant to you as a professional learner as to your students as learners. Be actively in charge of your learning and take appropriate actions. Make your professional development work for you. Of course your professional development programme leaders, trainers and mentors will guide and support you in your learning, but you are at the heart of your own learning experience, not on the receiving end of something that is cast in stone. Those who assist and advise you on your professional development want you and your colleagues to get the best out of the experience, and need your feedback along the way so that if necessary they can adapt and improve what they are devising.

## 2  Challenge
*In principle*

Reflection is a constructive process that helps the individual teacher to improve their thinking and practice. It involves regularly asking questions of yourself about your developing ideas and experience, and keeping track of your developing thinking, for example in a reflective journal. Reflection is continuous, rather than a one-off experience. Being honest with yourself means thinking hard, prompting yourself to go beyond your first thoughts about a new experience and to avoid taking for granted your opinions about something to which you are accustomed. Be a critical friend to yourself.

In the Cambridge PDQ Certificate in Teaching and Learning, for example, teachers take a fresh look at the concepts and processes of learning and challenge their own assumptions. They engage with theory and models of effective teaching and learning, and open their minds through observing experienced practitioners, applying new ideas in practice and listening to formative feedback from mentors and colleagues. To evidence in their assessed portfolio how they have learnt from this experience, they not only present records of observed practice but also critical analysis showing understanding of how and why practices work and how they can be put into different contexts successfully.

The Cambridge PDQ syllabuses set out key questions to focus professional learning and the portfolio templates prompts to help you. These questions provide a framework for reflection. They are open-ended and will not only stimulate your thinking but lead to lively group discussion. The discipline of asking yourself and others questions such as 'Why?' 'How do we know?' 'What is the evidence?' 'What are the conditions?' leads to thoughtful and intelligent practice.

## Approaches to learning and teaching Science

*In practice*

Challenge:

- Yourself, as you reflect on an experience, to be more critical in your thinking. For example, rather than simply describing what happened, analyse why it happened and its significance, and what might have happened if conditions had been different.
- Theory – by understanding and analysing the argument, and evaluating the evidence that supports the theory. Don't simply accept a theory as a given fact – be sure that you feel that the ideas make sense and that there is positive value in applying them in practice.
- Convention – the concept of 'best practice(s)' is as good as we know now, on the basis of the body of evidence, for example on the effect size of impact of a particular approach on learning outcomes. By using an approach in an informed way and with a critical eye, you can evaluate the approach relating to your particular situation.

### 3  Share

*In principle*

Schools are such busy places, and yet teachers can feel they are working on their own for long periods because of the intensity of their workload as they focus on all that is involved in teaching their students. We know that a crucial part of our students' active learning is the opportunity to collaborate with their peers in order to investigate, create and communicate. Just so with professional learning: teachers learn best through engagement with their peers, in their own school and beyond. Discussion and interaction with colleagues, focused on learning and student outcomes, and carried out in a culture of openness, trust and respect, helps each member of the community of practice in the school clarify and sharpen their understanding and enhance their practice.

This is why the best professional learning programmes incorporate collaborative learning, and pivotal moments are designed into the programme for this to happen frequently over time: formally in guided learning sessions such as workshops and more informally in opportunities such as study group, teach meets and discussion, both face-to-face and online.

*In practice*

Go beyond expectations!

In the Cambridge PDQ syllabus, each candidate needs to carry out an observation of an experienced practitioner and to be observed formatively themselves by their mentor on a small number of occasions. This is the formal requirement in terms of evidence of practice within the portfolio for the qualification. The expectation is that these are not the only times that teachers will observe and be observed for professional learning purposes (rather than performance appraisal).

However, the more that teachers can observe each other's teaching, the better; sharing of practice leads to advancement of shared knowledge and understanding of aspects of teaching and learning, and development of agreed shared 'best practice'.

So:

- Open your classroom door to observation
- Share with your closest colleague(s) when you are trying out a fresh approach, for example an idea in this book
- Ask them to look for particular aspects in the lesson, especially how students are engaging with the approach – pose an observation question
- Reflect with them after the lesson on what you and they have learnt from the experience – pose an evaluation question
- Go and observe them as they do the same
- After a number of lessons, discuss with your colleagues how you can build on your peer observation with common purpose, for example lesson study
- Share with your other colleagues in the school what you are gaining from this collaboration and encourage them to do the same
- Always have question(s) to focus observations and focus these question(s) on student outcomes.

**Pathways**

The short-term effects of professional development are very much centred on teachers' students. For example, the professional learning in a Cambridge PDQ programme should lead directly and quickly to changes in the ways your students learn. All teachers have this at heart – the desire to help their students learn better.

The long-term effects of professional development are more teacher-centric. During their career over, say, 30 years, a teacher may teach many thousand lessons. There are many good reasons for a teacher to keep up-to-date with pedagogy, not least to sustain their enjoyment of what they do.

Each teacher will follow their own career pathway, taking into account many factors. We do work within systems, at school and wider level, involving salary and appointment levels, and professional development can be linked to these as requirement or expectation. However, to a significant extent teachers shape their own career pathway, making decisions along the way. Their pathway is not pre-ordained; there is room for personal choice, opportunity and serendipity. It is for each teacher to judge for themselves how much they wish to venture. A teacher's professional development pathway should reflect and support this.

It is a big decision to embark on an extended programme of professional development, involving a significant commitment of hours of learning and preparation over several months. You need to be as clear as you can be about the immediate and long-term value of such a commitment. Will your programme lead to academic credit as part of a stepped pathway towards Masters level, for example?

Throughout your career, you need to be mindful of the opportunities you have for professional development. Gauge the value of options available at each particular stage in your professional life, both in terms of relevance to your current situation – your students, subject and phase focus, and school – and the future situation(s) of which you are thinking.

# Understanding the impact of classroom practice on student progress

Lee Davis, Deputy Director for Education,
Cambridge International Examinations

14

# Introduction

Throughout this book, you have been encouraged to adopt a more active approach to teaching and learning and to ensure that formative assessment is embedded into your classroom practice. In addition, you have been asked to develop your students as meta-learners, such that they are able to, as the academic Chris Watkins puts it, 'narrate their own learning' and become more reflective and strategic in how they plan, carry out and then review any given learning activity.

A key question remains, however. How will you know that the new strategies and approaches you intend to adopt have made a significant difference to your students' progress and learning? What, in other words, has been the impact and how will you know?

This chapter looks at how you might go about determining this at the classroom level. It deliberately avoids reference to whole-school student tracking systems, because these are not readily available to all schools and all teachers. Instead, it considers what you can do as an individual teacher to make the learning of your students visible – both to you and anyone else who is interested in how they are doing. It does so by introducing the concept of 'effect sizes' and shows how these can be used by teachers to determine not just whether an intervention works or not but, more importantly, *how well* it works. 'Effect size' is a useful way of quantifying or measuring the size of any difference between two groups or data sets. The aim is to place emphasis on the most important aspect of an intervention or change in teaching approach – the **size of the effect** on student outcomes.

Consider the following scenario:

Over the course of a term, a teacher has worked hard with her students on understanding 'what success looks like' for any given task or activity. She has stressed the importance of everyone being clear about the criteria for success, before students embark upon the chosen task and plan their way through it. She has even got to the point where students have been co-authors of the assessment rubrics used, so that they have been fully engaged in the intended outcomes throughout and can articulate what is required before they have even started. The teacher is happy with developments so far, but has it made a difference to student progress? Has learning increased beyond what we would normally expect for an average student over a term anyway?

Here is an extract from the teacher's markbook.

| Student | Sept Task | Nov Task |
|---|---|---|
| Katya | 13 | 15 |
| Maria | 15 | 20 |
| Joao | 17 | 23 |
| David | 20 | 18 |
| Mushtaq | 23 | 25 |
| Caio | 25 | 38 |
| Cristina | 28 | 42 |
| Tom | 30 | 35 |
| Hema | 32 | 37 |
| Jennifer | 35 | 40 |

**Figure 14.1**

Before we start analysing this data, we must note the following:

- The task given in September was at the start of the term – the task in November was towards the end of the term.
- Both tasks assessed similar skills, knowledge and understanding in the student.
- The maximum mark for each was 50.
- The only variable that has changed over the course of the term is the approaches to teaching and learning by the teacher. All other things are equal.

With that in mind, looking at Figure 14.1, what conclusions might you draw as an external observer?

You might be saying something along the lines of: 'Mushtaq and Katya have made some progress, but not very much. Caio and Cristina appear to have done particularly well. David, on the other hand, appears to be going backwards!'

What can you say about the class as a whole?

# Calculating effect sizes

What if we were to apply the concept of 'effect sizes' to the class results in Figure 14.1, so that we could make some more definitive statements about the impact of the interventions over the given time period? Remember, we are doing so in order to understand the size of the effect on student outcomes or progress.

Let's start by understanding how it is calculated.

An effect size is found by calculating 'the standardised mean difference between two data sets or groups'. In essence, this means we are looking for the difference between two averages, while taking into the account the spread of values (in this case, marks) around those averages at the same time.

As a formula, and from Figure 14.1, it looks like the following:

$$\text{Effect size} = \frac{\text{average class mark (after intervention)} - \text{average class mark (before intervention)}}{\text{spread (standard deviation of the class)}}$$

In words: the average mark achieved by the class *before* the teacher introduced her intervention strategies is taken away from the average mark achieved by the class *after* the intervention strategies. This is then divided by the standard deviation[1] of the class as a whole.

---

[1] The standard deviation is merely a way of expressing by how much the members of a group (in this case, student marks in the class) differ from the average value (or mark) for the group.

# Understanding the impact of classroom practice on student progress

Inserting our data into a spreadsheet helps us calculate the effect size as follows:

| | A | B | C |
|---|---|---|---|
| 1 | Student | September Task | November Task |
| 2 | Katya | 13 | 15 |
| 3 | Maria | 15 | 20 |
| 4 | Joao | 17 | 23 |
| 5 | David | 20 | 18 |
| 6 | Mushtaq | 23 | 25 |
| 7 | Caio | 25 | 38 |
| 8 | Cristina | 28 | 42 |
| 9 | Tom | 30 | 35 |
| 10 | Hema | 32 | 37 |
| 11 | Jennifer | 35 | 40 |
| 12 | | | |
| 13 | Average mark | 23.8 = AVERAGE (B2:B11) | 29.3 = AVERAGE (C2:C11) |
| 14 | Standard deviation | 7.5 = STDEV (B2:B11) | 10.11 = STDEV (C2:C11) |

**Figure 14.2**

Therefore, the effect size for this class $= \dfrac{29.3 - 23.8}{8.8} = 0.62$

But what does this mean?

# Interpreting effect sizes for classroom practice

In pure statistical terms, a 0.62 effect size means that the average student mark **after** the intervention by the teacher, is 0.62 standard deviations above the average student mark **before** the intervention.

We can state this in another way: the post-intervention average mark now exceeds 61% of the student marks previously.

Going further, we can also say that the average student mark, post-intervention, would have placed a student in the top four in the class previously. You can see this visually in Figure 14.2 where 29.3 (the class average after the teacher's interventions) would have been between Cristina's and Tom's marks in the September task.

This is good, isn't it? As a teacher, would you be happy with this progress by the class over the term?

To help understand effect sizes further, and therefore how well or otherwise the teacher has done above, let us look at how they are used in large-scale studies as well as research into educational effectiveness more broadly. We will then turn our attention to what really matters – talking about student learning.

# Effect sizes in research

We know from results analyses of the Program for International Student Assessment (PISA) and the Trends in International Mathematics and Science Study (TIMMS) that, across the world, a year's schooling leads to an effect size of 0.4. John Hattie and his team at The University of Melbourne reached similar conclusions when looking at over 900 meta-analyses of classroom and whole-school interventions to improve student learning – 240 million students later, the result was an effect size of 0.4 on average for all these strategies.

What this means, then, is that any teacher achieving an effect size of greater than 0.4 is doing better than expected (than the average) over the course of a year. From our example above, not only are the students making better than expected progress, they are also doing so in just one term.

Here is something else to consider. In England, the distribution of GCSE grades in Maths and English have standard deviations of between 1.5 and 1.8 grades (A*, A, B, C, etc.), so an improvement of one GCSE grade represents an effect size of between 0.5 and 0.7. This means that, in the context of secondary schools, introducing a change in classroom practice of 0.62 (as the teacher achieved above) would result in an improvement of about one GCSE grade for each student in the subject.

Furthermore, for a school in which 50% of students were previously attaining five or more A*–C grades, this percentage (assuming the effect size of 0.62 applied equally across all subjects and all other things being equal) the percentage would rise to 73%.

Now, that's something worth knowing.

# What next for your classroom practice? Talking about student learning

Given what we now know about effect sizes, what might be the practical next steps for you as a teacher?

Firstly, try calculating effect sizes for yourself, using marks and scores for your students that are comparable, e.g. student performance on key skills in Maths, reading, writing, Science practicals, etc. Become familiar with how they are calculated so that you can then start interrogating them 'intelligently'.

Do the results indicate progress was made? If so, how much is attributable to the interventions you have introduced?

Try calculating effect sizes for each individual student, in addition to your class, to make their progress visible too. To help illustrate this, let us return to the comments we were making about the progress of some students in Figure 14.1. We thought Cristina and Caio did very well and we had grave concerns about David. Individual effect sizes for the class of students would help us shed light on this further:

| Student | September Task | November task | Individual Effect Size |
|---|---|---|---|
| Katya | 13 | 15 | 0.22* |
| Maria | 15 | 20 | 0.55 |
| Joao | 17 | 23 | 0.66 |
| David | 20 | 18 | -0.22 |
| Mushtaq | 23 | 25 | 0.22 |
| Caio | 25 | 38 | 1.43 |
| Cristina | 28 | 42 | 1.54 |
| Tom | 30 | 35 | 0.55 |
| Hema | 32 | 37 | 0.55 |
| Jennifer | 35 | 40 | 0.55 |

* The individual effect size for each student above is calculated by taking their September mark away from their November mark and then dividing by the standard deviation for the class – in this case 8.8.

**Figure 14.3**

If these were your students, what questions would you now ask of yourself, of your students and even of your colleagues, to help you understand why the results are as they are and how learning is best achieved? Remember, an effect size of 0.4 is our benchmark, so who is doing better than that? Who is not making the progress we would expect?

David's situation immediately stands out, doesn't it? A negative effect size implies learning has regressed. So, what has happened, and how will we draw alongside him to find out what the issues are and how best to address them?

Why did Caio and Cristina do so well, considering they were just above average previously? Effect sizes of 1.43 and 1.54 respectively are significantly above the benchmark, so what has changed from their perspective? Perhaps they responded particularly positively to developing assessment rubrics together. Perhaps learning had sometimes been a mystery to them before, but with success criteria now made clear, this obstacle to learning had been removed.

We don't know the answers to these questions, but they would be great to ask, wouldn't they? So go ahead and ask them. Engage in dialogue with your students, and see how their own ability to discuss their learning has changed and developed. This will be as powerful a way as any of discovering whether your new approaches to teaching and learning have had an impact and it ultimately puts data, such as effect sizes, into context.

# Concluding remarks

Effect sizes are a very effective means of helping you understand the impact of your classroom practice upon student progress. If you change your teaching strategies in some way, calculating effect sizes, for both the class and each individual student, helps you determine not just *if* learning has improved, but by *how much*.

They are, though, only part of the process. As teachers, we must look at the data carefully and intelligently in order to understand 'why'. Why did some students do better than others? Why did some not make any progress at all? Use effect sizes as a starting point, not the end in itself.

Ensure that you don't do this in isolation – collaborate with others and share this approach with them. What are your colleagues finding in their classes, in their subjects? Are the same students making the same progress across the curriculum? If there are differences, what might account for them?

In answering such questions, we will be in a much better position to determine next steps in the learning process for students. After all, isn't that our primary purpose as teachers?

# Acknowledgements, further reading and resources

This chapter has drawn extensively on the influential work of the academics John Hattie and Robert Coe. You are encouraged to look at the following resources to develop your understanding further:

Hattie, J. (2012). *Visible Learning for Teachers – Maximising Impact on Learning.* London and New York: Routledge.

Coe, R. (2002). *It's the Effect Size, Stupid. What effect size is and why it is important.* Paper presented at the Annual Conference of The British Educational Research Association, University of Exeter, England, 12–14 September, 2002. A version of the paper is available online on the University of Leeds website.

The Centre for Evaluation and Monitoring, University of Durham, has produced a very useful effect size calculator (available from their website). Note that it also calculates a confidence interval for any effect size generated. Confidence intervals are useful in helping you understand the margin for error of an effect size you are reporting for your class. These are particularly important when the sample size is small, which will inevitably be the case for most classroom teachers.

# Recommended reading

15

# 15 Approaches to learning and teaching Science

The resources in this section can be used as a supplement to your learning, to build upon your awareness of Science teaching and the pedagogical themes in this series.

**For a deeper understanding of the Cambridge approach, refer to the Cambridge International Examinations website (www.cie.org.uk/teaching-and-learning) where you will find the following in-depth guides:**

*Implementing the curriculum with Cambridge;* a guide for school leaders.

*Developing your school with Cambridge;* a guide for school leaders.

*Education briefs* for a number of topics, such as active learning and bilingual education. Each brief includes information about the challenges and benefits of different approaches to teaching, practical tips and lists of resources.

*Getting started with ...* These are interactive resources to help to explore and develop areas of teaching and learning. They include practical examples, reflective questions and experiences from teachers and researchers.

For further support around becoming a Cambridge school, visit www.cambridge-community.org.uk.

## The nature of the subject

Driver, R., Squires, A., Rushworth, P. & Wood-Robinson, V. (2014) *Making Sense of Secondary Science: Research into Children's Ideas.* London: Routledge.

Oversby, J. (2012) *ASE Guide to Research in Science Education.* Hatfield: Association for Science Education.

Wellington, J. & Ireson, G. (2012) *Science Learning, Science Teaching.* London: Routledge.

## Key considerations

ASE (2006) *Safeguards in the School Laboratory.* Hatfield: Association for Science Education.

Abrahams (2010) *Practical Work in Secondary Science: A Minds-On Approach.* Continuum.

Cambridge International Examinations (2015) *Guide to Planning Practical Science.* Cambridge: Cambridge International Examinations.

## Interpreting a syllabus

ASE (2016) *The Science Leaders' Survival Guide*. Hatfield: Association for Science Education.

## Active learning

Osborne, J. (2010) *Good Practice in Science Teaching: What Research Has to Say*. London: Open University Press.

Reiss, M., ed (2011) *Teaching Secondary Biology* (2nd edition). London: Hodder Education.

Sang, D., ed (2011) *Teaching Secondary Physics* (2nd edition). London: Hodder Education.

Taber, K., ed (2011) *Teaching Secondary Chemistry* (2nd edition). London: Hodder Education.

## Assessment for Learning

Keeley, P. (2008) *Science Formative Assessment: 75 Practical Strategies for Linking Assessment, Instruction, and Learning*. California: Corwin/NSTA Press.

Wiliam, D. (2011) *Embedded Formative Assessment*. Bloomington, IN: Solution Tree.

## Metacognition

Abrahams, I., Reiss, M. eds (2017) *Enhancing Learning with Effective Practical Science 11–16*. New York: Bloomsbury.

Dunlosky, J. (2013) Strengthening the Student Toolbox: Study Strategies to Boost Learning. *American Educator* 37:3; 12–21. Available online on the American Federation of Teachers website.

Hattie, J. (2009) *Visible learning: A synthesis of 800+ meta-analyses on achievement*. Oxford: Routledge.

Millar, R., Le Maréchal, J-F. & Tiberghien, A. (1999) 'Mapping' the Domain: Varieties of Practical Work. In: Leach, J. & Paulsen, A., eds, *Practical Work in Science Education: Recent Research Studies* (pp. 33–59). Roskilde/Dordrecht: Roskilde University Press/Kluwer.

## Language awareness

Naylor, S., Keogh, B. & Mitchell, G. (2000) *Concept Cartoons in Science Education*. London: Millgate House.

Mercer, N. (1995) *The Guided Construction of Knowledge. Talk Amongst Teachers and Learners.* London: Multilingual Matters.

Mercer, N. (2000) *Words and Minds. How We Use Language to Think Together.* London: Routledge.

Wellington, J. & Osborne, J. (2001) *Language and Literacy in Science Education.* London: Open University Press.

### Inclusive education

Gershon, M. (2013) *How to Use Differentiation in the Classroom.* London: Create Space Independent Publishing.

Ross, K., Lakin, L., McKechnie, J. & Baker, J. (2015) *Teaching Secondary Science.* London: Routledge.

Hudson, D. (2015) *Specific Learning Difficulties – What Teachers Need to Know.* London: Jessica Kingsley Publishers.

### Teaching with digital technologies

Mazur, E. (2013) *Peer Instruction, New International Edition.* Harlow: Pearson.

Ross, J. (2011) *Online Professional Development: Design, Deliver, Succeed!* California: Corwin.

### Global thinking

Hammerman, E. (2006) *Eight Essentials of Inquiry-Based Science.* California: Corwin.

Butterworth, J. & Thwaites, G. (2013) *Thinking Skills: Critical Thinking and Problem Solving.* Cambridge: Cambridge International Examinations.

Llewellyn, D. (2013) *Teaching High School Science Through Inquiry and Argumentation.* California: Corwin.

### Understanding the impact of classroom practice on student progress

Watkins, C. (2015) *Meta-Learning in Classrooms.* The SAGE Handbook of Learning. Edited by Scott, D. and Hargreaves, E. London: Sage Publications Ltd.

# Index

Abrahams, Ian, 19
access
    providing, 98–99
    to learning activities, 99
active learning, 6
    approach, 31–32
    challenges of
        incorporating, 32
    definition of, 31
    facilitating, 38–39
    group work, 36
    in Science, 33
    students' prior ideas, 33
    thinking, 37–38
    through inquiry, 40–42
    working out ideas for
        themselves, 34–36
advocates, 121
AfL. See Assessment for
    learning (AfL)
alternatives, 52
analyse, 41
annotated photos illustrating
    gravity, 107
argument writing frame, 124
argumentation, 123–125
assessment
    objectives, 25
    of prior knowledge, 47
    type and nature of, 25–26
assessment for learning
    (AfL), 6, 44
    asking useful questions, 52–53
    challenges of
        incorporating, 45
    definition, 44
    effective feedback, 53–54
    eliciting understanding and
        generating discussion,
        49–50
    responsive teaching, 50–52
    starting point, 47
    success, 46
    usage of, 44–45
assumptions, 52
auditory access, 98
autonomy, 13

balloon debate, 120
behaviour, 94–96
bilingual dictionaries, 82
    of scientific laboratory
        equipment, 83
Bloom's Taxonomy, 92
body of knowledge, 10, 11, 59

cartoon, 75, 76
challenging, 135–136
chance to help, 89
children with
        misconceptions, 10
clarification, 52
class experience, 61
classroom, 88
    activate peers as educational
        resources, 88
    chance to help, 89
    change your plans, 89
    culture of learning in, 58
    experience success, 89
    practice on student progress,
        140–142
    starting points of your
        students, 88
    students learning, 88
    technique, 49
CLIL. See Content and
    language integrated
    learning (CLIL)
cognition, 96–98
    strategies, 96–97
collaboration, 127
command words, 38
communication, 41, 93–94, 127
    strategies, 93–94
conceptual learning, 19
connect, 41
consequence mapping, 123
consequentialism, 125
constructing, 78
content and language
    integrated learning
    (CLIL), 72
controversial issues, 120–122
Cornell note-taking method, 65

creative recording, 65
creativity, 127
critical thinking, 128
curriculum, 5, 9–10, 19

data collection, 11
differentiation
    by outcome, 91
    by route, 91
    by task, 90–91
    thinking about, 90–92
digital filing cabinet, 104–105
digital technologies, teaching
    with, 7, 102
    challenges of using, 102–103
    definition of, 102
    digital filing cabinet, 104–105
    flipped learning, 111
    learning, then choose, 104
    online professional
        development, 114–115
    picture tells story, 105–107
    simulations and
        visualisation, 112–113
    using technology to capture
        data, 107–109
    using technology to
        process and present data,
        109–110
    working together, 113
distillation apparatus, 105
divergent thinking, 127
drama, 120

EAL. See English as an
    additional language (EAL)
economies, fundamental
    components of, 9
education, 5
effect sizes
    calculating, 142–143
    in research, 144–145
    interpreting, 143
effective feedback, 53–54
effective learners/learning, 6,
    61–63. See also Learning
    formation of, 5

emotional development, 94–96
English as an additional
    language (EAL), 72
envoys, 77
ethical decisions, 9, 125–126
evaluation, 61
evidence, 40, 52
exemplar long-term plan, 28
exit ticket, 46
experimental-based learning, 9
explain, 41

facilitating, 38–39
feedback, 44, 53–54
    quality of interactions and, 44
    techniques, 54
flash card testing, 66
flipped learning, 111
focusing, 133–135

global thinking, 6, 117, 129
    about controversial issues,
        120–122
    approach, 117–118
    argumentation and inquiry,
        123–125
    challenges of
        incorporating, 118
    definition of, 117
    in Science, 119
    making ethical decisions,
        125–126
    problem-solving and
        practical learning, 126–129
good questions, 53
group work, 36
    fit for purpose, 36
    member, 36
    outcomes, 36

highlighting, 78
hinge-point, 50, 52
holistic appreciation of
    learning, 6
hot seating, 121

implication, 52
inclusive education, 7, 86–87
    challenges of, 87
    classroom (See Classroom)
    definition of, 86
    importance, 87
    overcoming barriers to
        learning (See learning)

thinking about
    differentiation, 90–92
ingenuity, 127
initiation, 82–83
innovation, 127
inquiry, 40–42, 123–125
    structuring learning
        through, 41
inquiry-based learning, 9
interaction, 93–94
interaction strategies, 93–94
intuitive sense-making, 10
inventiveness, 127

jigsaw, 77

knowing, 11
    choices, 60–61
knowledge, 6, 19
    assessing prior, 47
    fundamental areas of, 10–11

labelling, 78
language, 7. See also Language
    awareness; Learning
    level, 22
    of Science, difficulties with,
        72–74
language awareness, 7, 70
    and Science learning, 72
    challenges of, 71
    definition of, 70
    difficulties with language of
        Science, 72–74
    initiation, 82–83
    orientation, 83
    reading, 78–79, 84
    speaking, 83–84
    talk, 74–77
    teachers, 70
    writing, 79–81, 84
learning, 5, 92–93
    barriers to, 6
    behaviour, emotional and
        social development, 94–96
    cognition and learning,
        96–98
    communication and
        interaction, 93–94
    conceptual, 19
    holistic appreciation of, 6
    implications of, 6
    in steps, 63–64
    language, 7

objectives, 25
processes of, 5
Science, 14
sensory, physical and
    medical needs, 98–100
strategies, 96–97
listening triads, 77
lively debate in class, 121

mantle of expert, 121
mark schemes, 79
matching, 78
mathematical skill level, 21–22
medical needs, 98–100
medium, 7
metacognition, 6
    definition of, 56
    evaluation phase, 57
    knowing choices, 60–61
    learning in steps, 63–64
    phases, 56–57
    planning phase, 56
    practical work, effective
        learning and
        self-evaluation, 61–63
    questions and, 67–68
    reflection phase, 57
    revising, 66–67
    revision and, 60
    Science, 59
    skills, 57–58
    taking notes, 65
metacognitive learners, 57
metacognitive techniques, 57
misconceptions, 34
mitosis, 106
monitoring, 61

news media, 120
non-consequentialism, 125

online professional
    development, 114–115
orientation, 83

pacing, 28–29
pair talk, 76
participation, 95
pathways, 137–138
peer instruction, 111
peer-work technique, 50
physical access, 98
physical needs, 98–100
picture, 105–107

planning, 61
positive behaviour, 95
practical learning, 126–129
practical work, 50, 61–63
    effectiveness of, 61
predicting, 78
problem-solving, 126–129, 128
professional learning, 17
progression of ideas, 64

questions, 40, 67–68
    for learning, 92

radioactive dice, 110
rainbow, 77
reading, 78–79, 84
recording, 78
reflect, 41
reflection, 128
reflective practice, 132–133
    challenging, 135–136
    focusing, 133–135
    pathways, 137–138
    sharing, 136–137
Reiss, Michael, 19
research evidence, 57
resilience, 13, 128
resources, 35
    special, 20
responsive teaching, 50–52
revising/revision, 66–67
    and metacognition, 60
    checklists, 64
risk-taking, 128
roles, 50

science
    curriculum, 9–10
    fundamental areas of
        knowledge, 10–11
    importance of, 13–14
    knowledge, methods and
        ways of knowing, 59
    learning, 72
    processes of, 11
    syllabus, 11
    why should students study,
        14–15

scientific development, 9
scientific language, 22
    initiation, 82–83
    orientation, 83
    reading, 84
    speaking, 83–84
    writing, 84
scientific learning, 36
scientific thinking, diversity
    of, 11
scientist, 12–13
secondary research, 48
self-evaluation, 61–63
self-confidence, 64
sensory needs, 98–100
sequencing, 78
sharing, 136–137
simulations, 112–113
skills, 9, 57–58
smart-phone features, 108
social development, 94–96
Socratic questioning, 52
soundtrack, 80
speaking, 83–84
special resources, 20
specialism, 18–19
spokesperson, 77
structure reasoning, 80
structuring and scaffolding
    learning
    pacing, 28–29
    think long term, 26–27
    think medium term, 27–28
structuring learning through
    inquiry, 41
students, 5, 17, 22–23
    choices, 60
    encouraging, 12
    fundamental to educating, 12
    involvement, 96
    language level, 22
    learning, 88, 145–147
    mathematical skill level,
        21–22
    prior ideas, 33
success, 89
syllabus
    aims, 25

assessment objectives, 25
    learning objectives, 25
    structuring and scaffolding
        learning (See Structuring
        and scaffolding learning)
    type and nature of
        assessment, 25–26
systematic 'sense-making', 10

taking notes, 65
talk, 74–77
teachers, 7, 70
    practical work, 19
    specialism, 18–19
teaching, 5
    and learning strategies, 45
    practice, 17
    processes of, 5
    responsive, 50–52
    special resources, 20
    through everyday
        contexts, 98
    understanding, 17
    use questions, 17–18
    with digital technologies
        (See digital technologies,
        teaching with)
    work out ideas for
        themselves, 18
teamwork, 50
thinking, 11, 37–38
    about differentiation,
        90–92
    command word, 37
Toulmin's framework for
    argument, 123
TV chat show, 120

videos, 111
visual access, 98
visualisation, 112–113

ways of knowing, 59
wheelchair-accessible
    laboratory bench, 99
Wiliam, Dylan, 52
working together, 113
writing, 79–81, 84

37523379R00090

Printed in Great Britain
by Amazon